Working with conflict in social work practice

Working with conflict in social work practice

Brian Littlechild, with Karen Mills
and Rose Parkes

Open University Press

Open University Press
McGraw-Hill Education
8th Floor, 338 Euston Road
London
England
NW1 3BH

email: enquiries@openup.co.uk
world wide web: www.openup.co.uk

and Two Penn Plaza, New York, NY 10121-2289, USA

First edition published 2020

A catalogue record of this book is available from the British Library

ISBN-13: 9780335248360
ISBN-10: 0335248365
eISBN: 9780335248377

Library of Congress Cataloging-in-Publication Data
CIP data applied for

Typeset by Transforma Pvt. Ltd., Chennai, India

Praise Page

This is a well organised book, written in a clear style. It contains much helpful material to assist social work students, social workers and their managers when dealing with an important aspect of social work practice - conflict as experienced in a wide variety of settings and situations. Sound attention is given to the structural, legal, organisational and individual aspects of conflict in social work, with the helpful provision of extensive references, many key learning points, numerous reflective exercises and constructive recommendations for the use of additional resources.

Stewart Collins, Honorary Research Fellow, Bangor University

In addressing the issue of conflict in a range of social work settings, this accessible text will have a broad appeal. It will be of particular interest to social workers during their education and training and in the early stages of their careers. Clearly written, with the inclusion throughout of reflective exercises and signposts to a broad range of additional material, this book will also be a very valuable resource for social work educators and managers.

Dr Martin Kettle, Senior Lecturer and Programme Lead,
Glasgow Caledonian University

"This is a welcome and valuable contribution to the social work library. It draws on years of accumulated wisdom and practice knowledge to help social work practitioners negotiate the contentious territory of conflict and challenge. These are inevitable features of practice, and the wise and expert guidance that this book offers is only too welcome".

Roger Smith, Professor of Social Work, Durham University

Social workers practice in a liminal place between their employers and people on the margins of society. Littlechild and his colleagues offer sage and practical advice for dealing with challenges across a range of social work fields. Whilst conflict often arouses fear it can be used positively to engender new, emergent ways of being. This positively framed book provides welcome insights and presents these accessibly and confidently. A must for the beginning social worker.

Dr Jonathan Parker, Professor of Society &
Social Welfare, Bournemouth, UK

Social workers often need to balance their ability to support individuals, while also exercising their responsibilities to keep an individual, or others safe. In this context conflict can arise about both the aims and practise of

social work. In this well written and carefully crafted book the authors have sought to help readers to contextualise conflict, offering advice and guidance about how to respond in ways which are likely to be constructive. The book is a wonderful resource, underpinned by a clear set of values, with helpful exercises to support reflection and learning. I've enjoyed reading it and learned a lot, and I expect others will do so too.

Professor John Devaney, Centenary Chair of Social Work, University of Edinburgh

This text eloquently and concretely addresses the often challenging and messy area of social work practice - working with conflict. Covering the full array of social work practice from direct work to managing the work environment, this text is filled with tools, strategies, and practical approaches to protecting oneself as a social worker and the service users and carers with whom they work.

Barbra Teater, Professor of Social Work, College of Staten Island, City University of New York

To Carole, Brian's very understanding and supportive wife, and Tom, our lovely and engaging son – thank you both for all the wonderful times.

Preface

This book is the result of my career-long interest, as a social worker, as to how social workers can best be supported, in what can be extraordinarily challenging and stressful (as well as extraordinarily rewarding) work. Equally, however, it comes from a concern about what can be a disempowering, stressful and challenging world for many service users and carers.

It is perhaps not hard to understand how social work service users and carers, who are having at times to deal with enormous pressures in different ways in their lives, might respond to social work interventions with avoidance and/or aggression. This is particularly so when we take into account the unique areas of social work in terms of our dual role of care and control, and of having to balance the often conflicting rights and needs of all those involved in a situation.

It reflects my belief that it is our duty as social workers to determine how we can best understand and work with these challenges that affect our own professional – and sometimes our personal – lives, as well as the challenges our service users and carers face.

My sincere hope is that this book may in some small way help to make the lives of ourselves as social workers, and of our service users and carers, safer and more satisfying.

Contents

Contributors

Brian Littlechild is Professor of Social Work at the University of Hertfordshire. His practice background is in mental health, looked-after children, child safeguarding and work with young people who have offended. He has carried out a number of research projects in relation to violence, conflict and work with involuntary service users, and has published a number of books and articles, and delivered conference papers nationally and internationally, in these areas. Brian has been carrying out training and consultancy in the areas of violence and work with involuntary service users for over 30 years.

Karen Mills is Principal Lecturer in Social Work at the University of Hertfordshire and leads the MSc Social Work and Step Up to Social Work programmes. Her practice background is in probation. Karen's research interests include substance misuse, and diversity and child safeguarding. She has over 25 years' experience in teaching and practice education, supporting student learning and developing reflective practice on pre-qualifying programmes.

Rose Parkes is Deputy Head of Higher Education (Academic and Applied Programmes) at University College Jersey. She also leads the island's newly created degree in social work. Her practice experience is in criminal justice, having worked for the probation service in the UK prior to joining academia in 2005. Her current doctoral study seeks to evaluate prison yoga.

1 Introduction

This book provides a resource for social workers and social work students in understanding the causes of conflict in social work, and in providing effective responses to the various types of conflict you may experience. The book provides knowledge, strategies and practice development ideas concerning the types of conflicts that may arise in your work, and how best to try to deal with these for the benefit of both yourself and your service users.

In this introduction we will address why conflict in social work settings is a problem, what types of conflicts you might encounter, from whom, and in what sort of circumstances. The book will explain how you can best recognize and work with a range of areas that can cause conflict. This includes reluctant service user engagement, resistance, and oppositional behaviours; aggression, threats, abuse and physical violence; and abusive and harassing behaviours directed against people with disabilities. It also covers issues of sexism, racist behaviours, where someone is being targeted because of lesbian, gay, bisexual, transgender, queer/questioning + (LGBTQ+) status, and bullying and harassment. In addition, it examines areas where the conflict is with colleagues, fellow students, managers or other professionals.

A key cause of conflict with service users and carers is the complex and multi-layered roles we undertake in many social work settings, and our skilled and delicate balancing of care and control, safeguarding and empowering. Social workers are among the most skilled professionals in dealing with conflicts, because of the experience that we have as a result of our work remit. We involve ourselves in the personal challenges of service users, as well as in the wider formal and informal systems of involving service users, carers and others. Unlike most other professions, we are often involved in having to address the rights and needs of the different people involved in a situation, often in challenging and distressing circumstances.

The Oxford English Dictionary defines 'conflict' as 'A serious disagreement or argument, typically a protracted one; A state of serious incompatibility between two or more opinions, principles, or interests.' Such conflicts, defined in this way, then relate to the dual role in social work, which means that sometimes you have to deny people what they would like, need or wish for, for example in terms of gatekeeping of resources, refusing what people believe you should give them, or in relation to safeguarding children and adults. The key issue of how we balance up the rights of those different people involved includes ourselves, and our rights to safety and well-being at work. These are examples of where there can be a conflict of interest between you and the service user, but also between the different members of the family themselves. Issues of confidentiality and information sharing, particularly with other agencies involved in interprofessional working, and when we maintain this or breach it, are also important areas of potential conflict.

The book examines what you should expect of yourself and your agency, whether you are a student social worker, newly qualified social worker, more experienced social worker or at managerial level.

Aims of the book

The aims of this book, then, are to provide readers with knowledge and practical guidance on how to assess and deal with the different forms of conflict experienced by social work staff. Some staff have to cope with such behaviour on a daily basis – for example verbal abuse – while others may only have to deal with it rarely but the nature of it may have serious outcomes.

This emphasis is not meant to be a depressing take on our work: quite the opposite. I have always tried in my teaching for students and training for social workers to emphasize that in order to understand and deal with this area effectively, we need to appreciate how service users may see our role, putting ourselves into thinking how they may experience our interventions. This is key to understanding and developing effective, open and honest relationships with service users which can lead to outcomes that are realistic, achievable and safer for service users, carers and social workers.

The book will examine how to identify the types of conflict that arise in social work, and why these may occur in different arenas and settings – for example:

- with service users and carers (the term 'service user' is used throughout the book, and may also include issues for carers in relation to the points being discussed; if the point is specific to carers, that is the term that will be used)
- in conflict between service users and carers
- with colleagues/managers
- with practice educators/tutors
- with other students
- with others in interprofessional working

If you are in the middle of a difficult situation face to face with service users and carers, it will explain how you can best try to calm things down or remove yourself from the conflict appropriately; or if conflict has happened, what you can best do, when, and how to deal with the aftermath most positively for yourself, service users and carers, and then try to avoid it happening again.

By the end of the book, it is intended that you will be more confident in recognizing the types of situations where there is risk of conflict, and where and why these may occur; in using effective responses to these risks in terms of your individual approaches as a practitioner; and in knowing how best to gain support in this from within your staff group and agency.

The learning from the book is intended to be able to be applied to all settings in social work and social care, including safeguarding children and vulnerable adults' work, mental health work, work with people with learning disabilities, and work with older people. Each chapter will address what you should expect of yourself, and of agency support for you.

Key elements from the Social Work England professional standards (2019a) in relation to these issues will be covered in the chapters, along with relevant key areas from the knowledge and skills statements for social workers of the Chief

Social Worker for England for Adults (Department of Health 2015) and the Chief Social Worker for Children (Department for Education 2018b).

Key points: what the book offers for your practice

The book will help you to consider issues about, and to work with:

- how you can best try to recognize and assess the risks of conflicts in situations you may become involved in
- how you can then best plan to avoid conflict
- how you can best deal with this in face-to-face situations if it does happen
- if conflict has happened, how you can best consider your responses personally and in what you can expect from your employers
- how you can best consider what happened, why, and try to prevent it happening again

The nature of social workers' relationships with service users

A key area of social work and social care work is to strive to base our relationships with service users on an empowering approach, with co-production of assessments, plans and services, within as optimistic an approach as we can. It is fundamental to social work that we believe that our work can help service users, and work with their problems and find ways to deal with their stress, disadvantage and conflict in their living situations and in their relationships (Wilson et al. 2011). However, given our clear knowledge about the incidence and effects of different forms of violence, abuse and aggression from service users, and various forms of resistance – including knowledge of the effects on service users themselves and others in their families and wider communities – if we do not address these problems, we are ignoring these effects, which can have powerful and disempowering effects on all involved. We need to balance these areas of risks with our other more collaborative and empowering values and aims.

Social work is, if it is about anything, about relationships (Megele 2015). The deeply respectful and validating elements of how we engage with, and respond to, service users' and carers' needs and difficulties are key issues in any set of human relationships. This is particularly important for social work as many of our service users and carers are from among the most disadvantaged and discriminated against in our society. The way that various forms of unfair discrimination can combine, and the effects of this, are discussed later in this chapter.

As Megele puts it, social work is at the sharp end of society's fears, anxieties and traumas, and intervenes in people's lives at points where they may be overwhelmed by emotions and distress, with the subsequent loss of equilibrium and homeostasis. Many service users and carers may have been or are currently subject to abuse, and suffer stress and distress in disempowering relationships and situations. They may feel that they experience this stress and distress in the face of your agency's take on social work roles. They may be struggling with problems and difficulties that negatively affect their sense of self and their experiences – therefore, the relationship-based practice of social work becomes an essential core component of social work knowledge and practice (Ruch 2012). However, this core element of striving for empowerment of service users and strength-based approaches can also be a problem due to the aggressive and resistant motivations of a small minority of service users and carers. This is where there may be a problem in terms of our understanding and use of our knowledge about the 'rule of optimism' (see more on this in Chapter 4) – this can mean that in certain situations we are not always so good at dealing with issues of conflict with service users and carers, such as resistance, violence, aggression, harassment and abuse.

The sets of attitudes and behaviours social workers can understand and make use of are important for the service users and carers in such situations, as they may be concerned about, or even fearful of, how social workers may judge them, and what the outcomes of our assessments and interventions might be. Therefore, in terms of our approaches, some key concerns are about being honest in our role of care and control, in balancing up the rights of all involved, such as in some areas of child/adult safeguarding and mental health work; and not being able to promise confidentiality, as explored in Chapter 10.

Recognizing that you may have power, authority and control in some if not all of your social work roles, and how service users and carers experience these, requires you to take into account your professional role and your agency function, as delivered from within your own personal style, background and previous learning.

It also means considering these matters for service users and carers from within their own individual areas of learning, attributes and behaviours, from an appreciation of cultural issues, and of transactional issues between yourself and the service users and carers.

Reflective exercise: what can cause conflict

When reading each chapter, in relation to the areas of conflict explored in the book, consider what issues you think there might be between:

1. yourself and your service users
2. yourself and your colleagues/managers/practice educator

In your work with these groups, think through some of the issues that may have affected actual or potential conflict, and how you might approach them differently having considered the issues raised in that chapter.

For those who might be presenting behaviours that you think lead to conflict with you, consider how you can best understand the situation from both your own and their perspectives.

Service users and carers' attitudes and attributions

Issues of empowerment and service user involvement in decision-making and plans are key to social work (see e.g. Beresford 2012; Byers and Creating Links

2013; Creating Links 2019). However, at times, service users and carers may not be able or willing to cooperate or agree with the way staff and agencies work with them. They may object to or find threatening for a variety of reasons the ways in which staff approach them, and/or the services they are or are not being offered. They may take exception to the roles you have to carry out – particularly in terms of the control elements of the work which you must carry out alongside your caring functions as a social worker. The Social Work England standards state that as a social worker I must '*recognise and use responsibly, the power and authority I have when working with people, ensuring that my interventions are always necessary, the least intrusive, proportionate, and in people's best interests*', and '*Promote social justice, helping to confront and resolve issues of inequality*'. However, in addition they state that as a social worker I must '*Recognise the risk indicators of different forms of abuse and neglect and their impact on people, their families and their support networks*', and '*Recognise and respond to behaviour that may indicate resistance to change, ambivalent or selective cooperation with services, and recognise when there is a need for immediate action*'.

In order to meet these conflicting demands, it is suggested in this book that is best to, as far as possible, acknowledge and agree our role and the purpose of assessments and interventions with service users and carers, within co-production and shared decision-making of plans to the greatest extent possible. We can look at this goal as sitting at the top of the ladder of conflict resolution approaches introduced in the next section. However, if this cannot be made to work, then we need to acknowledge this, taking full account of how the service user and others see the issues, thus openly recognizing the conflict, and using a solution-focused, problem-solving approach in order to agree a way forward.

Within this, we need to use more assertively authoritative approaches, where we need to make clear what our role from within our agency is, and how we propose to move forward with service users at least having knowledge of why we are doing what we are, even if not necessarily with their full (or indeed at times any) consent and cooperation. This open and shared agenda involves agreeing plans with them, the methods we use, and the outcomes that we are looking for in relation to the intervention. Elements of this can be used even if it might not be possible to fully agree processes and outcomes with them, but where your reasons for your views and actions have been made clear in terms of your role within your agency function. For example, in rare events in areas such as mental health work under the Mental Health Act 1983, adult safeguarding under the Care Act 2014, and child safeguarding work within the Children Acts, we may need to be on the bottom rung of the ladder where we are obliged to enact these legislative requirements.

Hierarchy of engagement

The ladder in Table 1 is set out with ways to avoid conflict, based on social work values, to be striven for first, before we go down the list only if needs be.

Key to positive engagement in trying to avoid conflict is our set of skills in listening and reflecting, in empathy and in projective understanding of service

Table 1 Hierarchy of engagement

1) Best approaches from an inclusive perspective: consensual agreement with service users	The hallmark of this level is shared decision-making on issues to be addressed, and how this is done, for example using task-centred approaches. There is agreement with the service user on what their issues and concerns are; setting out clearly what your role is, and the aims and means to achieve them; and how and by when you will each do what is agreed, then jointly review the effectiveness of the plan, with the criteria to gauge this.
2) Engaging with a partly consensual/engaging person – this may be where you are having to consider using controlling or coercive measures to some extent, e.g. resource restriction, domestic violence, safeguarding or Mental Health Act 1983 issues start to come into play	Consensus on issues to be addressed and how this will be done, as above, even though there are tensions and some level of disagreement on this. Agree with service user and/or carer what their issues, concerns and disagreements are concerning your assessment/intervention. Set out clearly what your role is, the aims and means to achieve what you have to, and why; how and by when you will review plans as to their effectiveness, and the criteria this is based on.
3) Engaging with the non-consensual/non-engaging/aggressive person	Set out with the service user or carer your understanding of what their issues and concerns are; what your role and aims are, why, and means you will have to take to achieve them. This may be where you are using coercive/controlling/restrictive/rationing measures to some level, for example safeguarding or Mental Health Act 1983 interventions. Even if there can be no agreement about these areas, you still need to aim to be as open and honest as possible about your concerns. You may also need to start considering how you will protect yourself from aggressive and abusive behaviours at this stage.
4) When protective demands override the above strategies	You have to make ethically and legally sound decisions where there is a need to take coercive actions, possibly sharing information with the professional network involved without consent or even sometimes the knowledge of the service user, where you need to balance the rights and needs of all involved. Social workers have to define/determine what needs to be acted on, and how, still within being open and honest as soon as possible. Where there are threats and aggression or abuse against you, you need to consider actions to take to resolve these issues and to make sure you are protected – see Chapter 11 for a hierarchy of responses to such behaviours.

users' concerns. This is important in order to try to achieve the best outcomes with both service users and carers, within an understanding of when we may need to look out for situations where we cannot achieve full consent for our methods and goals, and how then to take matters to the next best approach.

The approaches to be aimed for are at the top of the table, with descending preferences, down to absolute necessity at the bottom.

Using this approach as a base, the aim of this book is to examine the causes and effects of different forms of motivations and behaviours relating to conflicts in social work and social care settings, and how best to respond to such behaviours in personal, team and agency contexts. In order to do this, we need to understand the thinking, motivations and attributions towards social work and social care roles from service users' perspectives, as well as those of front-line staff and managers, and have an appreciation of these different actors' perceptions, positions and their understanding of the transactions between them. In turn, we need then to develop insights on how to understand the context of the work undertaken, and how this affects the experience of service users and ways they may respond to being under scrutiny, as experienced by them, and the resistance they may respond with, and why.

Reflection point

Your main aims in these areas of work should be to anticipate, from an understanding of your own approaches, and the views of the conditions/motivations/experiences of service users and carers, how perceived and actual power differentials and views of issues may lead to conflict and possibly aggression in assessments and interventions. You can aim to make these openly acknowledged areas, in order to deal with them as well as possible within social work approaches and values, using the ladder of conflict resolution approaches set out in Chapter 11 to engage with service users/others, and to produce recognition/agreement on these matters as best you can.

Intersectionality issues

How people may experience our agency services and our personal approaches is a key theme of the book for us to consider in our practice relationships. One overarching question for this is our understanding and use of intersectionality (Mattsson 2013; Bubar et al. 2016), where different elements of unfair discrimination can combine to impact the lived experiences that may affect all groups of service users and carers.

Intersectionality by definition encompasses a number of factors that may affect people's access to and experiences of services, including among others LGBTQ+ and areas of disabilities (for discussion of the Equality Act on these areas, see Chapters 6 and 9; and on issues of how domestic violence overlaps with these issues, see Chapter 7).

The International Federation of Social Workers' (IFSW) statement relating to intersectionality is:

> *Structural barriers contribute to the perpetuation of inequalities, discrimination, exploitation and oppression . . . reflecting on structural sources of oppression and/or privilege, on the basis of criteria such as race, class, language, religion, gender, disability, culture and sexual orientation, and developing action strategies towards addressing structural and personal barriers are central to emancipatory practice.*
>
> (IFSW 2014)

Key points: Intersectionality

An understanding of intersectionality and how to use it in practice is important for social workers in order to deliver our values. This helps us to think proactively about each area of potential disadvantage and unfair bias/discrimination, from within which service users and carers may experience our assessment and interventions, and the possible interconnected and multiplying effects of having more than one of these characteristics/disadvantages.

This chapter now examines one of these areas in detail in relation to Black, Asian and Minority Ethnic groups, as an exemplar of how we might take such matters into account.

Exemplar: Black, Asian and Minority Ethnic (BAME) groups

In England, people from Black, Asian and Minority Ethnic groups are more likely to live in deprived areas and be poorer (ESRC Centre on Dynamics of Ethnicity 2013; Child Poverty Action Group 2019). Social work, health and social care systems can then amplify and compound these inequalities. Examples of this can be found in the disproportionate number of people from ethnic minorities, particularly people from certain BAME groups, within the control elements of, for example, mental health work such as being sectioned under the Mental Health Act 1983, and the child safeguarding and youth justice systems (Littlechild 2012; LankellyChase Foundation 2014; Gov.uk 2017).

In order to understand different BAME communities' experiences of mental health problems and of services provided, it is also necessary to consider the 'intersectionality' of other aspects of identity and shared social circumstance such as gender, age, religion, disability, health and location (LankellyChase Foundation 2014), and LGBTQ+ issues.

Reflective exercise

How might you, if you were a person from a BAME group, experience and/or be concerned about social work interventions? How might this affect how motivated/encouraged/able you might be to work with the social worker and their services?

Imagine the person's thoughts, feelings and attributions towards the social worker, taking into account their likely experiences of wider social experiences and possibly oppression, and your agency policies, resources and procedures.

What would you want in a social worker in terms of their skills/attitudes in ways of communicating with you, planning the assessment and intervention, and reviewing progress?

'Othering'

Ben-Ari and Strier (2010) argue that the French philosopher Emanuel Levinas's conceptualization of the 'Other' – where certain groups are seen as inherently inferior, as the Nazis did with the Jewish people – challenges conceptions of cultural competence, arguing that we need to examine the relationship between this concept and the 'Other'. Cultural competence is where social workers understand and respond positively to cultural differences. Having cultural competence means having the ability to appreciate the experiences of, communicate with and work effectively with people from, for example, different cultures/ethnicities (Littlechild 2012). This is only one part of the story though; in addition, we need to understand the more generic factors – such as unfair discriminatory views about someone because they are part of, for example, a faith or LGBTQ+ group – from a consideration of intersectionality and the types of issues that might apply to all service user groups.

Diversity, cultural sensitivity and cultural relativity

One key area in many countries for social work is that of anti-oppressive practice. In England the recognition of and strategies to identify oppressive practices in relation to people because of, for example their ethnicity, gender, LGBTQ+ status and so on, has been a key feature of social work practice and social work education for some 40 years, paving the way for this to have been recognized to some extent in other professions.

In terms of our understanding of, and approaches to, conflict in social work – a key element which relates the issue of projective understanding of the other person's experiences of social workers and their attributions to them – this then relates to any form of difference and diversity, such as in terms of gender, ethnicity, culture, faith, and sexual orientation.

Conflict situations can generate intense feelings, so it is important to be able to apply empathy and projective understanding to those feelings and to be able to work with them – an example of what has come to be known as '*emotional intelligence*' (Howe 2008).

Cultural competence is key to social workers' approaches, where social workers need to understand and positively respond to problematic areas in cultural differences. It can be argued that in order to expand our theoretical and practical framework for working with difference, a comprehensive understanding of the relations between 'Self' and the 'Other' is necessary (Ben-Ari and Strier 2010). Ben-Ari and Strier set out that social workers have a need to recognize how to respond effectively to people of all different cultures, ethnic backgrounds, religions, social classes, and indeed all 'Other' diversity factors. This means that social workers must be able to recognize and value the worth of individuals, families and communities, and protect and preserve the dignity of all. These issues are covered in more depth in Chapter 4 on work with children and families, in terms of balancing cultural sensitivity in cultural competence with cultural relativity.

These are important issues in relation to social work values and practice, and they are reflected in the Social Work England professional standards, which we now look at in terms of sections of the standards which relate to conflict in social work.

Key points: the elements of Social Work England's professional standards in relation to working with conflict

Social workers must:

1.2 *Respect and promote the human rights, views, wishes and feelings of the people I work with, balancing rights and risks and enabling access to advice, advocacy, support and services.*
1.6 *Promote social justice, helping to confront and resolve issues of inequality and inclusion.*
1.7 *Recognise and use responsibly, the power and authority I have when working with people, ensuring that my interventions are always necessary, the least intrusive, proportionate, and in people's best interests.*
2.1 *Be open, honest, reliable and fair.*
2.3 *Maintain professional relationships with people and ensure that they understand the role of a social worker in their lives.*
2.4 *Practise in ways that demonstrate empathy, perseverance, authority, professional confidence and capability, working with people to enable full participation in discussions and decision making.*

These points, in relation to being open and honest, including people as much as possible in discussions about assessments and plans, while also being authoritative and persevering, balancing up the rights of each of the people involved in a situation, and ensuring that service users understand the role of social workers in relation to their circumstances, are themes which are worked in throughout the discussions in this book.

The effects on social workers

The effects on social workers and social care staff who are having to cope with conflictual situations and behaviours can be personal, emotional and professional. These often go unrecognized or ignored by management, and in supervision, policies and procedures. Important though the effects on staff are, however, the book is not just about these effects on staff. If such behaviours are not recognized and planned for, the effects can be damaging for service users and carers, both psychologically and physically, such as in adult or child safeguarding work. This is also true in residential and day care, where if service users are not having positive work done concerning their behaviours which negatively affect others, we are not carrying out our duties to help them make a commitment to having more satisfactory relationships. Abuse, threats, harassment and the fear of violence affect not only the health and well-being of staff, but also workers' capacity to carry out their work effectively, and their commitment to that work.

The crossover of individual and agency issues

The balance of individual and agency responsibility is a key theme in the book. Each is interdependent on the other. How individuals respond to conflictual behaviours depends on several different and interlinked factors. So, in any particular situation, the balance of factors will vary – the presence of varying factors and how they relate to each other are key. Secondly, there is what the worker themself brings to their work and the situations they confront in the different areas of social work and social care. Such an approach then leads us to the possibility of engaging with a model for dealing with aggression, resistance and violence from service users as set out above. How we might best understand the relationship relevant to conflict between service users, carers and social workers is set out in detail in Chapter 2, with particular reference to ideas from transactional analysis (TA), the drama triangle and the Johari window.

The way we recognize, plan to minimize the risk of, and react to conflict on a personal level is multilayered. Issues personally for workers that can lead to conflict, for example our own previous learning and experiences of conflict, and the attitudes that we can then carry with us from these into our professional lives, are included. In addition, and in tandem with this set of understandings, are external factors such as stress from the work – including how well supported we feel at work in relation to these areas, and how comfortable we feel in being able to be assertive in demanding support in relation to them. This then needs to include consideration of the culture in which we are working, and the attitudes and behaviours of others and how these could be managed. Issues of how best to support staff and implications for personal practice in such conflict situations are addressed throughout.

The structure of the book

The chapters in the book include features to help highlight certain issues and learning opportunities based on critical self-reflection, such as the use of *Key points*, *Reflection points* and *Reflective exercises*. The chapters include links to additional resources, some of which are freely available as videos on You Tube. The ones recommended are those that may be most useful, but they may sometimes be taken down; if that happens, please do a search on You Tube with keywords from that section to come up with alternatives that you might find useful for yourself.

Chapter 2 addresses generic approaches to assessment of, and effective methods of working with, conflict in social work. It introduces readers to ways that can be used to assess and respond to different types of conflict, including transactional analysis, the drama triangle and the Johari window, which provide means to further understand both ourselves and service users and carers, within the use of non-aggressive assertiveness. The development of projective understanding of other people's views of us in our roles, from the other person's point of view, is included, as is the value of using task-centred approaches and motivational interviewing.

Chapter 3 covers areas of conflict with specific service user groups, and looks at how individuals experiencing mental health challenges, learning disability services, autism spectrum condition, and older people's services may experience and view social workers, which can lead to situations of conflict with them. These issues may include rationing of services, where carers' and service users' interests and wishes may conflict, and where conflict may arise due to service users' responses to their concerns and/or fears about the roles social workers carry out, such as in the Approved Mental Health Practitioner role.

Chapter 4 is concerned with the issues of working with parents in safeguarding children work, and with looked-after children. The chapter examines threats of violence as well as resistance and disguised compliance from parents. It addresses issues of cultural sensitivity as well as cultural relativity. There is examination of what we can take into account in relation to the experiences and attributions towards social workers of looked-after children, in how they may see us in our social work role, and how we can relate with young people in ways which can encourage them to trust social workers.

Chapters 5 deals with how best to assess risk of, and respond at personal and agency levels to, physical violence and threats. It includes discussion about how our communications with service users may exacerbate or diminish the risk of such violence taking place. The chapter looks at practical measures for predicting what may happen, what to do in the situation, and afterwards.

Chapter 6 addresses abusive behaviour, such as sexual/racist/disablist/LGBTQ+ abuse and harassment from service users and carers, in terms of our personal practice and what support we should expect from employers over this, based on their legal duties and responsibilities.

Chapter 7 addresses conflict between service users and carers, covering areas of domestic abuse and violence, and issues of conflict arising from safeguarding issues when social workers intervene in relation to such work for children and vulnerable adults. Behaviour involving abuse and control in relationships between service users and carers is not uncommon, and the effects on the victims can be very disempowering and physically, emotionally and socially damaging.

Chapter 8 is concerned with recognizing and working positively with conflict on social work qualifying courses where conflict arises between students. The way in which this chapter is structured is different from other chapters in the book, as there is little previous work in this area. It is therefore based on a case study which critically analyses the issues involved in learning from a situation of conflict between students. (Conflict for students within placements and their universities, with practice educators, tutors and colleagues in placement agencies, is dealt with in Chapter 9, in the same format as for the rest of the book chapters.)

The chapter evaluates how the conflict between students was dealt with, along with the ways in which such potential conflicts can be proactively addressed in social work qualifying programmes.

Recognizing and working with conflict in workplace/student practice learning settings, and addressing relationships with social workers' colleagues and managers are the concerns of Chapter 9. This chapter also includes the issues arising from the relatively new area of the duty of whistle-blowing when there are concerns which have not been addressed to a sufficient extent to protect the interests and safety of service users and carers by agencies.

Chapter 10 then examines the potential for conflict in interprofessional and interagency working. This will include looking at the key areas of status issues between the professions, and information sharing.

Chapter 11 discusses methods of how best to respond to conflicts, over and above what you can do as a social worker in your own personal practice. This includes, for example, mediation, restorative conflict resolution and critical incident analysis to aid risk assessment and risk management planning.

The concluding Chapter 12 summarizes key issues arising from the discussions in the book.

Additional resources

The four nations' professional standards on what social workers must work to, and be able to demonstrate that they are abiding by to stay registered, can be found as follows:

For England, see the Social Work England professional standards at https://socialworkengland.org.uk/professional-standards/ (accessed 29.02.20).

For Scotland, see the Scottish Social Services Council professional standards at https://www.sssc.uk.com/ (accessed 29.02.20)

For Wales, see the Social Care Wales professional standards at https://socialcare.wales/ (accessed 29.02.20)

For Northern Ireland, see the Northern Ireland Social Care Council professional standards at https://niscc.info/ (accessed 29.02.20)

For materials on relationship-based social work, including videos, see the Social Care Institute for Excellence guide at https://www.scie.org.uk/children/relationships (accessed 29.02.20).

2 Generic approaches to methods of working with conflict in social work

This chapter will introduce you to methods to assess and respond to different types of conflict, and how to apply these considerations in professional practice and student placements. It will look at ways which can help you be both empathetic and assertive in approaching the conflicts arising in different types of work with service users and carers, furthering your knowledge of individual personal responses, skills and strategies. At the same time, it acknowledges that you can only really best do this when it is nested – rather like Russian dolls – within effective first-line manager and staff group responses. This in turn needs to then be located within a supportive agency culture and, for social workers, within their professional registration body requirements. The chapter takes as its basis the model for hierarchy of engagement set out in Chapter 1, on how we can try to engage in the most open and honest way possible, and what we can do where this becomes problematic and conflict-laden.

The chapter will examine task-centred approaches with service users for dealing with conflict, and projective understanding of other people's views of yourself in your social work role. It will discuss use of approaches from transactional analysis, the drama triangle, the Johari window, non-aggressive assertiveness and motivational interviewing.

Conflict in social work relationships: a hierarchical approach

There is a hierarchy of what we should aim for in our relationships with service users and carers. This is to aim for the highest level of shared decision-making/co-production with service users and carers in terms of plans for and with them. Where you have attempted this to the best of your abilities, including using interprofessional networks, but you are not able to agree a way forward with the service user and/or carer about what the issues are and how to move forward together on them, you may need to move on to other approaches. In these circumstances, you can consider problem-solving approaches, setting out clearly the areas of disagreement, and considering these openly with service users and carers in how they apply to your work with them. When this in turn is not possible, with a minimum set of areas to be covered and how, to what purpose and what outcomes, then you may need to move on to the next level. This will either involve termination of contact and support, or where that may not be possible – for example, in relation to safeguarding issues – stepping further into the controlling elements of the social work role, to be implemented whether service users/carers agree or not, but still with the reasons for this being made clear.

Transactional analysis and the drama triangle

The value of transactional analysis (TA) in social work is that it is based on relatively simple concepts, as set out in the videos listed in the Additional resources section at the end of this chapter and in the works of Thomas Harris (2004) and Eric Berne (1964). I first became interested in TA early in my career following concerns about some limitations with the theories and methods I had been taught on my social work qualifying course. These seemed to have only limited value in relation to working as a newly qualified social worker in a local authority. A number of service users were reluctant to engage with my/our methods and offerings, and some could be aggressive, violent and highly resistant. None of this was covered on my, otherwise pretty sound, four-year course.

Undertaking work with a TA practitioner helped me to understand some of the processes I was going through in my relationships with service users in my social work role, and with colleagues and managers. I found that TA approaches do not need to use technical, expert language, which can distance/disempower service users, so it is easier to reach a better understanding about the dynamics of the service user–social worker relationship and the concerns, motivations and behaviours based on both the social worker's and service user's experiences and attributions, and therefore of the interactions between them.

TA moves away from the idea that there is an 'expert' who is able to interpret others' background, influences and feelings, and uses tools and ideas to develop a more open and negotiated discourse. This fits well with ideas of task-centred work and motivational interviewing. It can give us one means, among others, of reflecting on what we do, how we do it, and why, and so reduce the potential for conflict with service users and carers.

This links to the idea of the drama triangle (which was developed from transactional analysis), where, for example, depending on your own background and possible learned prejudices and often unconscious discriminatory views, you may find these lead to difficulties with service users and carers because of old unexamined views, and ways we come across in relation to gender identity, ethnicity, gender, class and so on. In order to fully reflect on our own views of, and prejudices towards, others, we need to understand our own influences, and how we might be alerted to strengths, and any potential problems, in these, and then manage them so they fit in with our social work values effectively. For instance, if I have been abused in my childhood, and I am working with an abuser, I may have reactions in terms of feeling uncertain about my role with them. The service user might also use their learning and behaviours to disempower and make me feel uncomfortable, or worse. I may also have processed some of these experiences through my Adult ego state (see below), and therefore know how to empathize appropriately to a valuable degree.

If I have grown up in a situation with powerful messages that people of a certain ethnicity are 'inferior' to myself, I may exhibit attitudes/behaviours which make someone feel I do not fully respect them, have not included them enough, or that I am discriminating against them. If I am a service user or carer and encounter these attitudes, I may then react in ways which can lead to problematic interactions. The BASW (2012, para. 40) Code of Ethics sets out how '*social workers should recognise their own prejudices*', acknowledging that social workers are subject to conscious and unconscious bias.

A further key feature is in using the approach of projective understanding, where, as the social worker, you have a duty to try to understand influences on, difficulties for, and motivations of the service users and carers you are working with and for. This can help you become more self-aware and be more sensitive to what may be happening in their experiences and motivations, providing a valuable conceptual framework and practical ways of examining your professional relationships with others. Such approaches can help you in looking at your own approaches that you bring as a human being to your work, and help you to reflect on how you are working within social work values with service users in the most democratic and sensitive way. This requires an understanding of any biases and prejudices in your views of others which may be contributing to potential conflicts, and disempowering service users and carers.

Using such ideas in your interactions with service users and carers, and with colleagues, you can more fully practise openness, honesty, inclusion and shared decision-making, but also need to consider how you can keep these in place to the greatest degree where you are able to, even when your own safety and well-being or those of others is being put at risk.

Transactional analysis and the three ego states

Transactional analysis uses the idea of three ego states: the Parent, the Adult and the Child. It has been written about in terms of how this may apply to social work (Pitman 1982, 1990). In applying these ideas in the different areas addressed in each chapter, the book will use several points of reference drawing on these key areas for the situations raised.

Mutually satisfying, positive relationships are helped by staying in our Adult ego state, in which we are able to recognize and understand when we may be in a 'good' or 'bad' Parent or Child ego state at any particular time. This in turn relates to which ego state our service user or carer is in at that time, and how this may affect the relationship we are building with them – positively or negatively. As part of this use of such methods, in terms of task-centred approaches, key issues then are about recognizing and explicitly acknowledging, in order to:

1. set out in an assertive and empathetic manner what the issues are, for both you and the service user
2. encourage and facilitate service users and carers to do the same
3. reach agreements on how, together, you can achieve the objectives from those different understandings you have each set out

In this way you can start to agree what the issues are, stating this clearly and recognizing potentially different viewpoints, and how you can move forward from this point to reaching agreed objectives in a positive manner, within the constraints acknowledged in the hierarchy of engagement model in Chapter 1.

The Parent ego state

The Parent part of us originates in our learned attitudes and beliefs from when we were young, usually through parents and/or other important and influential carers. This part of us is seen as being like a non-rewritable CD: it is permanently recorded within us, and even if in our Adult ego state we determine we will do something different in terms of behaviour, we can – and particularly when under stress or involved in conflictual situations – revert to what those important people said and did, as well as also possibly the way they said it and did it.

In my teaching, in discussing this subject, I have sometimes asked students to think about their own backgrounds and learning in their families or alternative care situations, and if they have anything in those experiences which they had determined that as adults they would not wish to do to their own children, if they have them. We then discuss what happens when, for example, life is very stressful – if they have found themselves reverting to the types of responses they had from their carers, saying the same sorts of things, and maybe in the same sort of tone; a number can recognize this in themselves. The idea of the Parent in transactional analysis is how we learn, in a powerful way, what can have positive (in Nurturing Parent mode) but also negative (in Critical Parent mode) influences on our approaches with others, and therefore our relationships. But this can also be made use of in terms of understanding these messages and how we can use them in our own reflections on our learning and behaviours, and modify them.

There are two elements to our Parent ego state.

The *Nurturing Parent* state encourages, is protective, and makes people feel recognized, valued, warm, safe and cared for: 'Thank you so much'/'That was really good'/'Aah, your picture/drawing is beautiful!'/'Come and give me a big cuddle'/'I love you very much'/'Haven't you done brilliantly!'

However, it is the motivation behind the words, and the way the words are said in the context of the relationship, which are also important.

The *Critical Parent* is the one that makes people feel small, inadequate, unworthy, not good enough: 'I should have expected you to do this so badly'/'You nasty little child'/'You are no good at anything'/'You have always been a problem to me'/'Nobody likes you, and no wonder'/'Nobody thinks you are worth anything'/'No matter how much I do for you, you just do not appreciate me and what I do for you.' If we are in our Critical Parent mode as a social worker, we can show judgemental views – either verbally and/or non-verbally – about others' behaviours and our views about them, in distanced and cold ways. So, instead of saying, 'We could see that as an area of concern. Can you see why?'; 'Can you tell me what was in your mind when you were doing this, and what else you might have done differently?'; 'The concerns are that . . . can we look at how we both see it, and look at how we can agree a way forward?', we say, from a frustrated, angry, judgemental Critical Parent stance: 'This is completely unacceptable! We've talked about this before and you still carry on doing it. You really have no idea what should be happening here, and what we need you to do. I'm going back to my office and we are going to take action on this.'

The Adult ego state

The Adult ego state can be seen to be like a computer processor – there are no judgements. In this ego state you are inquisitive, open and looking to understand and engage positively with others in their Adult ego state, or realize where they are engaging or responding problematically in their Parent or Child ego states.

The social worker has an open manner and posture, makes contact in an appropriate way without being overbearing verbally or non-verbally, and invites discussion and dialogue. When you are trying to identify ego states, attempt to see and feel what is being indicated by yourself and your service user/carer by way of non-verbal communications, as well as what is actually said.

The Adult ego state is an 'accounting' or 'computing' function which can draw on the resources of both Parent and Child, as well as trying to identify which of these ego states you are in, the ego state the service user is in, and the effects of this on your discussions and transactions. This can then enable you to take a different approach to try to avoid transactions becoming problematic, rather than productive. Phrases associated with the Adult state are: 'What do you think about . . .?'; 'I think, I realize, I see, I believe . . .'; 'In my opinion, it may be that . . .'; 'It seems to me that possibly . . .'; 'How about if we . . .'; 'What if . . .?'; 'What might be the outcomes if . . .?'; 'Please don't . . .' (if said in a confident and appropriately assertive way).

The Child ego state

When we are in our Child ego state, we could be in either *Free Child* or *Adapted Child*. It can be positive: so, in the Free Child, we can have fun – while not at the expense of others – where we can play, and relieve some of the stresses from being in the other ego states. However, when in the Child ego state, we may be cooperative with the person we are engaging with, based on our learning about how we can engage with others and trust them. If we are fortunate, we will have had experiences with parental figures that have enabled us to learn about how to engage with and trust others, from a position where we had trust in our parents/carers, felt they had our interests at heart, and could trust their motives and engagements with us. However, engaging from our Adapted Child state can be problematic and negative, and we may possibly be overly compliant or resistant. If, in our early years, we have felt controlled, put down or threatened by parents/carers, and made to feel bad by them, service users in Critical Parent may catch our Adapted Child and make us find it difficult to be in Adult and assertive.

Reflection point

Reflection points: assertiveness

- In communications with service users, workers may appear overly aggressive, or alternatively too passive and open to manipulation, abuse and bullying.
- When expressing yourself clearly and directly in your Adult, you increase your chances of getting a point across effectively. Assertive communication, therefore, leads to more positive interactions between participants.

Assertive behaviour does not mean trying to come out 'on top', 'win' a point, show who has most power, or is most 'clever' to put someone down in an encounter. If one person is trying to do this, and succeeds, this must 'put' someone else 'down', and this – for social worker or service user – is likely to mean they will harbour grievances, anger, even rage, and try to 'win' the next time, either by direct confrontation or harassment/bullying.

So, for example, if in our work with the service user we are frustrated with them about their seeming non-compliance or lack of progress, it is unlikely we will be able to engage their Adult. We may become inappropriately authoritarian, rather than appropriately authoritative. We may start using distancing and dismissive body language and eye contact, and use phrases such as 'This is really unacceptable . . .'; 'We have spoken about this so many times in the past, and we made it clear what needs to happen'; 'You are deliberately undermining this . . .'. The message these words give are from Critical Parent, that the person is not of worth and is unable to change; it is much more likely to engage their Adapted Child, which in turn may make them angry, resentful and aggressive from their own learning of their feelings as a child being caught in this situation.

In the following chapters, we will use these ideas – TA, the drama triangle, the Johari window, task-centred approaches, projective understanding – to aid understanding of the motivations and behaviours of ourselves and service users/carers, and how they may affect transactions between everyone involved. These need to be used within a commitment to respectful relationships with service users and carers, but balanced with the need to take account of how we appropriately challenge the service user's behaviour where it is negatively affecting others involved, including yourself and other staff. This can be, for example, in relation to relatives of people with certain types of mental health challenges, in safeguarding adults and children situations, and so on. For instance, Lord Laming talks about where we are working with parents in safeguarding children situations – while we want to help them to be the best parents for their children, as judged in our legislation, policy and child development theory, we need to have '*respectful uncertainty*'. So while we respect the person for who they are, we do not necessarily always believe what they are telling us, when it may be that they are covering up issues in relation to the vulnerabilities/abuse of others.

As these ideas are applied in the different areas addressed in each chapter, the book will use several points of reference, drawing on these key areas for the situations raised.

The drama triangle

The drama triangle is a model of dysfunctional human interaction based on TA, originally described by Stephen Karpman, who identified three roles acted out as

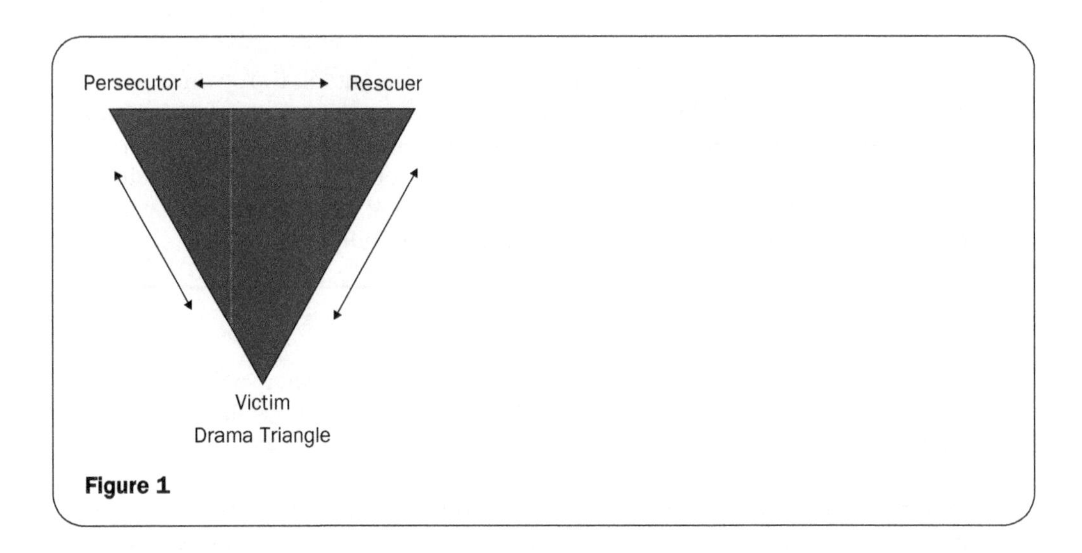

Figure 1

Persecutor, Rescuer and Victim (Burgess 2005; see Figure 1). For videos on this approach, see the Additional resources section.

The Rescuer and the Persecutor roles are shown at the top part of the triangle, as often it is seen that these roles assume a superior position over others. So, both Rescuers and Persecutors interact with others from the position that they are more confident, more competent, and of greater status than others.

TA ideas suggest that we all have a position on these three points which we tend to go to by default, normally learned from the situations in which we were brought up. If we are in Adult ego state, we can be aware that our Child and Parent ego states might be pushing us towards one of the points of the triangle where we do not want to be. Once we are on one of those points, the likelihood of switches being pulled to change from one to another is very high – with the usual position we end up in being Victim. If you determine to move away from being a Rescuer, you are likely to be seen as a Persecutor: 'How can you do this to me?'/'How dare you refuse to do this for me?', may be the responses of someone in Victim. If you are at the Rescuer point, this can move you into Persecutor if the other person does not play their role: 'What do you mean you don't need my help?' responses. In other words, to escape becoming the Victim, we must be willing to be perceived as the 'bad social worker'.

It is useful to consider how you might move between the three points, and eventually, as best you can, away from these roles in relationships, as otherwise there will always be 'switches' as to the one we are in, as the others involved are also moving between their roles. Self-awareness and critical reflection are then key to how you move forward. We may need to acknowledge and accept, for example, a tendency to rescue others, and understand that by rescuing (as I can tend to do) we are meeting our own needs, rather than genuinely helping others, and that it is possible to be supportive without rescuing.

Persecutors criticize and blame others. They may be in complete denial about their tactics and may argue that their behaviour is warranted and necessary for self-protection. They take a rigid, authoritarian stance and, like Rescuers, keep Victims in that role: 'Why won't you do what I have offered/advised?'

Victims take a default position of feeling and believing that they are oppressed, helpless, hopeless, powerless. This approach can prevent you or the service user taking responsibility for actions. In the Victim role, people often look for a Rescuer to engage with, who will ultimately compound their negative feelings about themselves. Social workers can often come from the Rescuer state – I think that I do, quite strongly – and we can sometimes try to 'take care' of service users to resolve problems for them. However, this can also infantilize them and put them into the Child state, from within which they may well end up feeling patronized, let down, that we did not respect them enough, get angry – and possibly be aggressive with us.

This model, then, relates to how assertive you can be in your work, which requires you to be in the Adult ego state. If you are not assertive, you can become a Victim, Persecutor or Rescuer. This is not good for the empowerment or personal development of service users, and not good for what is known about the types of relationships appreciated by them.

Key point: example of the drama triangle effects

In the case of the baby Peter Connelly, the Serious Case Review determined that the different agency workers involved saw the mother as the victim, while she was using her own past abusive experiences and current difficulties to set the agenda with workers so that they were not able to keep their focus on baby Peter and the abuse and neglect he was suffering. The serious case review determined that the mother had needed to be challenged and confronted about her poor parenting and generally neglectful approach to the home. The professionals, with all best intentions, seem to have been coming from Rescuer, and ended up in the Victim role.

Reflective exercise

Consider where you might most regularly start off, and then end up, on the three points of the drama triangle in your interactions with others, including service users and colleagues.

Do you tend to be a Rescuer, trying to make everything OK for everybody? Can you come across as a Persecutor in the way you may seem to judge service users and carers?

How often do you think you might become a 'Victim' as a result of becoming caught up in one of the other two points of the drama triangle?

The Johari window

The Johari window is a self-awareness tool with which we can try to better understand how we come across to others, in order to best judge how to use our knowledge of interactions, communication, diversity and empathy, as well as assertive approaches. This fits with Social Work England's professional standard to '*Incorporate feedback from a range of sources, including from people with lived experience of my social work practice.*' Skills for Care (undated a) has produced a guide for social workers on using this approach, with a particular focus on using it to audit their current level of capability – at the appropriate Professional Capabilities Framework (PCF) level – by reflecting on their practice and soliciting feedback from other team members and managers.

The Johari window is based on a diagram which looks like a four-paned window, and can be useful in helping us develop skills in empathy and cooperation, improving communications and group dynamics, and therefore our projective understanding. It takes into account feelings, views, attitudes, intentions and motivations in relation to four perspective 'areas'.

The size of the 'open area' can be expanded to the left into the self-unaware space, by seeking feedback and observations from service users and carers where this is at all possible. This is what we are doing when we ask service users and carers for feedback while students are on practice placements. It can also be valuable in enhancing your relationships with service users and carers by having open discussions about how we are viewing each other, and what you can learn

Table 2 The Johari window

Your self-unaware area	**Your open area**
(In the original model, it was known as the 'blind area'.) What is unknown by the person about him/herself, but which others know.	What is known by the person about him/herself and is also known by others.
The unknown area or unknown self	**The hidden area**
What is unknown by the person about him/herself and is also unknown by others – contains information, feelings, aptitudes, experiences etc. These unknown issues take a variety of forms: they can be reasons for feelings, behaviours, attitudes, and latent capabilities, influencing the person's behaviour to various degrees.	The hidden area is the information that you hide from others – consciously or unconsciously. This could include secrets, your past or current experiences or activities, feelings, thoughts, etc. Examples of hidden areas can include a fear, attribute or attitude that other people do not know you have – for example, messages in your Critical Parent about threats in various ways from people from BAME backgrounds and which in your Adult you may be working very hard to overcome, though those messages will always be there. Other examples may be about our sexuality, our age, if we have children or not, etc.

from this, to make use of in your work together. The size of the open area can also be expanded downwards into the hidden or avoided space by working with colleagues/supervisors that you feel you can trust and learn from in such open and honest discussions, with considered and appropriate disclosure of information and feelings, for example, about yourself to supervisors, colleagues, friends, managers, etc.

Even in difficult and conflictual situations, it can be valuable to discuss how you are seeing your role and what you are trying to do, with an equal emphasis on your sharing with service users and carers how you might see them and their behaviours in terms of the agreed areas of intervention. It is not only a way of appreciating how others see us and helping others see how they might be seen, but can be an important part of agreeing the tasks that you are both undertaking, for example as part of task-centred working.

Reflective exercise on the Johari window

- How do you/can you ask for/receive feedback on situations you have come across/been involved in to help you understand your own behaviours and change possibilities more, in order to consider in your Adult mode how you can monitor and deal with any potential biases from those messages that you will always carry around with you in your Parental mode?
- How easy do you find it to ask someone to give you feedback on how you have come across, and how good are you at listening to such feedback?

Reflective exercise: transactional analysis, the drama triangle and the Johari window

In your communications in direct work with service users, might you be appearing overly aggressive – or alternatively, too passive? Think about your and their positions in the three ego states, and how your positions in relation to the drama triangle might inform your learning about yourself and your interactions with others. How might the Johari window enable you to have greater understanding of these interactions and attributions, and projective understanding of the feelings, attributions and motivations of service users and carers?

Task-centred social work

Task-centred work can be valuable in the way it can help you think about how you agree your role and aims in assessments and interventions (Reid and Epstein 1972; Payne 2014). It was one of the first methods to be able to show effectiveness in terms of outcomes in the way plans were made, followed through and reviewed (Coulshed and Orme 2006; Sheldon and MacDonald 2009). Coulshed and Orme

(2006) suggest that task-centred work deals effectively with a number of areas, including for our purposes here interpersonal conflict, in order to improve satisfaction in social relationships in terms of role performance, and behavioural problems.

Trotter (2015) discusses how the use of task-centred work is of value with involuntary service users, and can be used alongside elements of behavioural approaches to give praise for small moves forward, and also prosocial modelling. This latter method can help where the behaviour and expressed attitudes of the service user are praised when the worker determines that prosocial behaviour is being exhibited, and therefore to be encouraged. At the same time, Trotter sets out how the worker can present the service user with a prosocial model by demonstrating respect and to some extent self-revelation, while also challenging antisocial behaviour and attitudes.

While it can be seen as a pure method, as with most social work methods, you can adapt it for your particular purposes – in this case, in relation to how you set up your relationship with the service user, based on openness and honesty to the greatest degree that you can, how you agree what you will focus on, how, and how and when you will review whether this is being effective or not.

For our purposes, this can be done in relation to where there may be issues of conflict, so that the social worker and the service user can discuss their perspectives on what the issues are, while the social worker does this from their perspective, with discussion about why these different perspectives exist, and agreement on what needs to happen, why, and when and how these will be reviewed.

Task-centred work is one of the methods which is seen to have the potential to empower service users the most, as it has moved social work towards problem-solving approaches based on open discussion and agreement with the service user about the issues and the ways to address them. This moved away from the idea that the person themself is inherently the problem, to looking at issues of concern, and openly discussing them as a way of dealing with difficult situations, then working on those issues – referred to as the target problem. It emphasizes moving towards the goals in a series of small steps, rather than expecting a global approach, which can be confusing, and allowing feedback in the behavioural sense in terms of giving praise when those small steps have been engaged with (Coulshed and Orme 2006). These approaches fit well with the hierarchy of engagement set out in the model in Chapter 1, and in the hierarchy of responses set out in the tables in Chapter 11.

Also, in terms of dealing with cultural and black and minority ethnic issues, task-centred work has been viewed as an important way of dealing with some of the issues in terms of cultural sensitivity, and as most amenable to the application of culturally sensitive and anti-oppressive practice (Devore and Schlezinger 1981; Milner and O'Byrne 2002).

Projective understanding

Projective understanding is a concept and method to understand what can be happening in relationships, and how we might empathize with others, while at the same time being aware of our social work role and what we are trying to achieve with the service user and/or carer. One useful set of ideas about this is referred to as 'emotional intelligence' by Howe (2008). If we are not able to do this, there is the risk that our responses and attributions lead to the situation escalating.

In order to do this, we need to think about how we develop and maintain our resilience, and think about this from our Parent/Adult/Child ego states, and from our understanding of ourselves from the Johari window and the drama triangle.

Reflective exercise on your use of TA, projective understanding and the Johari window

- 'What do you think your service users/carers/other professionals are bringing to their understanding of your role? And what might you yourself be bringing in from these areas to the situation?'
- What, from your own background learning, might you be bringing to these relationships in terms of bias, feelings, and therefore your approaches, which can affect our work in both positive and negative ways?
- What can you think of from your own Parent ego state messages and Adapted Child messages that can help you understand and process the messages from your Adult in order to most effectively engage with others from within social work values? How might this help you to provide the most effective assessments, interventions and reviews with service users about the work that you are doing on an open, honest and agreed basis?

Motivational interviewing

Motivational interviewing (MI) is a client-centred and directive approach. It was developed in the field of alcohol treatment and is now used in a wide range of areas. Of particular relevance here is that it has been used with positive results with involuntary service users (Anstiss et al. 2011), and has an evidence base (Forrester et al. 2012). Forrester et al. (2012) note how research findings emphasize the importance of the social worker being sensitive, honest and clear about social work procedures, and how in safeguarding children work, lack of ability to deal with service user resistance can mean that social workers may be inadvertently increasing the likelihood of problematic responses from the parents.

They also emphasize the importance of social workers demonstrating active listening and showing/checking with parents that they have correctly understood the latter's narratives; parents particularly appreciated workers who understood their perspective. Negative approaches observed from social workers occurred when they did not ask parents what their views and opinions were on their own situation. Forrester et al. argue for the value of motivational interviewing; having a focus on engaging parents; and a focus on eliciting 'change talk', a non-confrontational way of responding to discrepancies between what the service user is saying about the plan of work with them, and what you understand to be their wider goals or objectives, in order to resolve their ambivalence about behavioural change.

It can be important to encourage the service user to come up with possible solutions/alternative behaviours themselves, and not to be seen in Critical Parent in terms of telling them what to do (e.g. 'what would be the advantages of us working closely together for your child's welfare?').

Approaches in our ways of talking that can be helpful include:

- 'Can you tell me about what happened when . . .?' / 'How did you experience the . . .?' / 'Could you describe what led up to . . .?'/ 'How did you deal with that?'
- 'What were the thoughts that were going through your mind just before that, and at the time?'
- 'What changes have you/we seen?'
- 'In trying to move on/change, what problems have you encountered? What might have/would have helped?'
- 'Can you tell me the source of these problems?'
- 'Who has been most/least helpful to you during this time? Why?'
- 'How have they been helpful – or not?'
- 'Tell me about how your views/actions/behaviours have changed.'

Beware of taking an 'expert position', and reflect on whether your questions/ approaches promote engagement/change, or feel accusatory, blaming, dismissive or without hope. In addition, be wary of offering advice – be aware of this in interactions between your TA Parent and the service user's Child, and where this might end up for each of you on one of the three points on the drama triangle.

Conclusion

This chapter has been about trying to find ways to help us understand the situations and relationships we get involved in with service users, and why you and they might be doing what you/they are doing. This is with the aim of helping us work better, survive better and flourish at work, and so not take home the pressures and stresses that arise from the conflicts that have to be dealt with in social work, that can affect our practice, our own well-being, and that of friends and family.

Reflective exercise on your learning from this chapter

For each of the different types of aggression, resistance and conflictual behaviours identified in this book:

1. What elements from your own background/learning do you need to consider that may affect how you perceive and respond to different kinds of violence, resistance, abuse and aggression?

2. What may prevent you from being able to recognize the need for support and ask for support from your manager/colleagues/agency?
3. How can you increase your confidence in working with your team and first-line manager to ensure you have a more protective and supportive environment?

Additional resources

For an instructive video that helps with understanding the drama triangle and its effects, see https://www.bing.com/videos/search?q=Drama+Triangle+TED+Talks&&view=detail&mid=D0E4A302782CA0DE0033D0E4A302782CA0DE0033&&FORM=VRDGAR (accessed 17.04.20).

There are some good TED talks about transactional analysis and its use; see https://www.bing.com/videos/search?q=Transactional+analysis++TED+Talks&&view=detail&mid=E687F8D9C0346FB454F8E687F8D9C0346FB454F8&&FORM=VRDGAR https://www.bing.com/videos/search?q=Transactional+analysis++TED+Talks&&view=detail&mid=D1EB374B506A4C8E044BD1EB374B506A4C8E044B&&FORM=VRDGAR (accessed 17.04.20).

For some useful information on how to understand and make use of the Johari window, see for example https://www.skillsforcare.org.uk/Document-library/Social-work/Measuring-impact/Populated-johari-window.pdf http://learntech.uwe.ac.uk/CommunicationSkills/Default.aspx?pageid=1377 https://www.communicationtheory.org/the-johari-window-model/ (accessed 17.04.20).

3 Conflicts in social work with adult service user groups

This chapter will look at how certain individuals and groups of service users and carers may experience and view social workers, and how from their perspectives and experiences they may have attributions about you that can lead to situations of conflict with them. It covers areas of conflict in social work with individuals from several specific adult service user groups – those experiencing mental ill health, learning disability, autism spectrum condition or older people's services.

Understandings of how service users may view social workers' use of power, authority and control, as discussed in Chapter 1, are important in terms of appreciating how the individual you are working with might see you, due to their experience of social work's role in rationing services, its dual role containing control elements of the work alongside its caring functions, and in balancing the rights of each person where carers' and service users' and others' interests and wishes are in conflict. This means we need to consider how we can best manage our roles for people who have particular needs as a result of their experiences of services for their particular issues. This may include how – while our main concern is for the person's safety and well-being – we also have to take into account any issues of the (possibly contradictory) rights and interests of others.

Service users may have responded with anxiety or aggression to some of the tasks and roles we have to carry out, for example when we are undertaking the Approved Mental Health Practitioner role or undertaking admission to residential care. This chapter looks at how individual workers, staff groups and agency managers might best respond to these challenges.

Personal approaches

Within how you may be seen by service users in your social work role, it can be useful to consider how you might come across to them. Your Critical Parent messages/drama triangle positions may then be important, as these can affect the service user's Adapted Child, particularly if the person is in a vulnerable and/or aggressive state. A person's views about you, and their ways of interacting with you, will partly depend on what they have learned from the past in their experiences with you or previous social workers. For example, I may have concerns – or even fears – about approaching someone with mental health problems because I have powerful subliminal discriminatory messages from within my Critical Parent/Adapted Child that they will be violent towards me, or that they will be highly irrational. The same may be the case for someone from an ethnic minority group, where I may have unfair discriminatory and oppressive views from my Critical

Parent/Adapted Child ego state from my childhood experiences and learning which may cause distrust, distress, anger or resentment towards that person. This may then cause conflict due to my attitudes and approaches – not necessarily conscious on my part – as I may be presenting as dismissive, judgemental or oppressive due to my old, powerful messages about 'people from that group'.

Using the Johari window, I need to become more aware of how I might be experienced by the person I am working with, and from within the concerns they may have about me, so that I can try to have an appreciative projective understanding of their situation. In the same way, I need to be aware of how I might be seen within the drama triangle – as a persecutor? as a rescuer? – in how someone may be experiencing my use (as they perceive it) of power, authority and control. This is not to say that how I am perceived is always just down to me – the other person may equally have unfair messages causing them to judge/avoid me; I do need, however, to try to understand these different perspectives and to balance the possibilities about their stance against my own possible part in it too.

Key points: approaching service users and carers

In order to approach service users and carers where someone is from among the service user groups discussed in this chapter, it is important to be aware of:

- people's possible concerns and attributions about you in your role, including for example people from Black, Asian and Minority Ethnic (BAME) groups
- someone's history of involvement with our services in the past, how they experienced this at the time and how it may be affecting them now, including how that might relate to the types of conflicts that could arise between us

Reflective exercise: approaching possible conflict situations due to service users' attributions towards you in your social work role

How might you with sensitivity open up discussion on these issues, and communicate on how both of you can best work together to deal with the person's concerns, assure them you have their interests at heart, and how you will try to deal with difficult issues between yourselves that might arise?

Reflective exercise

Put yourself in the place of a person who has experience of:

1. mental health services – in particular of the coercive elements, such as involuntary admission to hospital under Mental Health legislation
2. dementia

3. learning disability services
4. autism spectrum condition
5. older people services
6. other service user groups you work with

For individuals from within each of these groups, imagine what the person's views, thoughts, feelings and attributions towards you in your role as the social worker may be, and how as the representative of your agency policies, resources and procedures, this may be experienced.

Consider what you, if you were a service user, would want from these considerations in how the social worker might approach/be with you? What issues might there be for you as a service user in being told about the social work role?

In terms of the social worker's ways of communicating with you, if you were a service user, what would you want from that social worker in the planning of the assessment and intervention, and reviewing how things are going?

Following on from these considerations of your and your service user's possible views and attributions towards each other, we now look at how some specific issues that may lead to conflict for certain groups may occur.

Mental health

In relation to the potentially coercive elements of mental health social work, for example involuntary admission to hospital, if you were to be in an Approved Mental Health Practitioner or similar role, it might be unsurprising for someone to feel an underlying level of concern and anxiety.

This could be exacerbated if someone suffers from depression and/or anxiety, or may be in a psychotic state, where there may be fear from within their perceived reality about someone else's motives and actions – while not being based in actual reality, it is very real for them, and will affect how they may react. (See Chris's, and actor David Harewood's, experiences of psychotic episodes, as set out in their videos on YouTube in the Additional resources section.)

Equally, if a parent has mental health problems, previous experiences may mean that they are fearful or resentful of what may happen as a result of interventions by social workers in this situation, leading to conflict in relation to aggression, or disguised compliance and resistance. They may well be concerned that they will be judged unfairly, from their perspective, because of the diagnosis they carry, such as personality disorder, schizophrenia, or depression and anxiety. If the parent/parents have some form of learning disability, or are known drug misusers, for example, the same concerns might apply.

In order to understand such issues in mental health areas – and this also applies to other areas addressed in this chapter – the National Institute for Health and Social Care (NICE), which provides evidence-based guidance and advice for health, public health and social care practitioners, has produced guidance on violence and aggression, examining how conflicts can arise in mental health work. It sets out the range of behaviours or actions that can result in harm, hurt or injury to another person. This is regardless of whether the violence or aggression is physically or verbally expressed, or physical harm is sustained. Its systematic review of the evidence found that violence and aggression are relatively common and can have serious consequences in health and social care settings. The manifestation of violence and aggression was found to be dependent on a combination of three key factors:

1. Intrinsic factors, such as intense mental distress and personality characteristics for individuals.
2. Extrinsic factors, including attitudes and behaviours of staff in patient ward or residential settings, and the attitudes and behaviours of other service users. This emphasizes the transactional nature of such conflicts and their prevention.
3. Physical settings, and any actual or perceived restrictions limiting a service user's freedom.

The guidance recommends that staff need to develop skills to assess when and why behaviour is likely to become violent or aggressive, including personal, constitutional, mental, physical, environmental, social, communicational, functional and behavioural factors that may be involved. It also states that staff need to develop more their skills, methods and techniques to try to avoid violence and defuse aggression when it arises. See Chapter 5 for more on this.

Particular issues for a service user with dementia might include why someone will not let them do something, and they hence feel unfairly controlled. The world for someone in this position can be inexplicable, threatening and very frightening. For carers, the loss of their relationship to a lesser or greater extent, and sometimes in the advanced stages of dementia aggression and resistance, present significant challenges, and can bring ongoing daily challenges, highlighting the need for support. See the Additional resources section for more on these areas.

Reflective exercise: conflicts within the family for the social worker to deal with

1. Imagine that you are working with a person suffering from dementia, who wishes to remain at home. They are living with other members of their family, but the family members' health and well-being are being severely undermined by caring for the person. Is it right to plan for the person to go to a residential unit, even though they cannot really fully consent to this, because you think it may be in their overall best interests, and in the best interests of the rest of the family?
2. How might each person be experiencing this situation from their own perspective, and how might you as the social worker take these perspectives into account and try to balance one against the others as far as possible?

Risks to self and others

One of the themes explored in this book is how social workers can try to balance the rights of the service user and the rights and needs of others. Research by Langan and Lindow (Langan 2000; Langan and Lindow 2004) into risk assessment from the perspective of how service users saw themselves in posing a risk to others provides insights into this area, and how to prevent conflicts that result from this. The research involved service users, relatives, friends, mental health and other community staff. The study's findings proposed that the most effective way of approaching risk assessments was to get to know the service user over time, and engage openly with them on their needs and the risks they may pose to themselves and others. This finding then leads us to consider how we can best build trust with service users, and how we can best engage in such potentially conflict-laden situations by way of being open and honest about our role, plans for assessment, and interventions. Such plans are best agreed where possible with the service user and possibly carers, following the hierarchy of engagement model set out in Chapter 1, in order to reduce the risk of conflict where this has not already happened, and taking into account concerns about the risks involved to self and to others, or in the aftermath of conflict.

At the same time, however, the study found that professionals are often concerned about being honest with service users, believing that honesty about risk assessments and consequent plans might generate concerning and aggressive behaviour. Hawley et al. (2006) and Littlechild and Hawley (2010) found that service users did not appear to be involved in their recorded risk assessments in NHS mental health trusts. This is an issue that needs to be addressed in practice, as it is counterproductive in terms of engaging and preventing conflict where professionals have made decisions and judgements without fully consulting/engaging with the service user.

Older people

There are particular issues for work with older people, particularly in relation to levels of need and the resources to meet these needs, even though we have the Care Act 2014 which sets out how personalized plans for care, focused on the well-being of the person, agreed with them and their carers, should be in place. The resources for such adult social care have been diminishing in recent years partly as a result of austerity, taking place at a time of increases in demand for care and health services due to an ageing population (Johnson et al. 2018). Increasingly having to be a gatekeeper, and ration or refuse resources where people cannot afford them themselves, will inevitably affect social workers' relationships with service users and their carers. This can be a cause for conflict when there are restrictions on services which the social worker knows are important for the health, well-being and safety of service users. Social workers can in turn have internal conflicts for themselves resulting from their frustrated feelings of wanting to provide for such needs of service users.

Learning disabilities

NICE, in its 2018 guideline on behaviour that challenges from children, young people and adults who have a learning disability, highlighted the role of cultural context in determining whether behaviour is perceived as challenging (Emerson 1995). In its guidelines on working with people with a learning disability and behaviour that challenges (NICE 2015a, 2018a), NICE recommends best ways to work with such behaviours, for the person themselves and family/carers, based on overarching principles that include working in partnership with children, young people and adults who have learning disabilities and behaviour that challenges, as well as their family or carers. These recommendations can also be applicable to other service user groups discussed in this book in order to reduce aggression and conflict. They are:

- Involve service users and carers in decisions about care.
- Support self-management and encourage the person to be independent.
- Build and maintain a continuing, trusting and non-judgemental relationship.
- Provide information about the nature of the person's needs, and the range of interventions (for example, environmental, psychological and pharmacological interventions) and services available to them, in a format and language appropriate to the person's cognitive and developmental level (including spoken and picture formats, and written versions in Easy Read style and different colours and fonts).

> **Reflective exercise: projective understanding of working with challenging behaviours**
>
> Imagine that you are working with someone with learning disabilities and/or mental health problems, aiming for them to have better relationships with carers, and greater presence/acceptance in society, but where they have challenging behaviours. How might you go about working with them in relation to these areas, taking into account the evidence-based guidelines from NICE?

Autism spectrum conditions

Autism spectrum condition (ASC), the term favoured by the National Autistic Society (undated), can mean that someone struggles with some aspects of everyday life, including forming friendships, coping at school or managing at work, that can often leave people with ASC confused, scared and overwhelmed. People with ASC may often struggle with vagueness or abstract concepts, which can cause great anxiety (National Autistic Society undated). Work by Simon Baron-Cohen (2011) demonstrated how someone who has an ASC may experience their world and how this may affect their capacity to have empathy for others, which may lead to conflict with and for them. A valuable account by someone who has an ASC is the book by Naoki Higashida (2013), which sets out graphically and succinctly how certain situations, experiences and elements in his environment can disrupt the order and predictability he needs in his life, causing great distress and uncertainty, and which can possibly lead to conflictual behaviours. Naoki highlights some of the issues he and other people with ASC may experience, with problems for them if the same things do not happen regularly at particular times. He also describes his experiences of social situations, which others need to be aware of when working with someone with an ASC, in order to sensitively meet their needs and also to try to avoid conflicts with them.

Conclusion

This chapter has examined how certain service user groups may experience the role of social work and social workers, with certain aspects which may contribute to or arise from issues particular to them. It has looked at how we might better understand the sets of relationships which can arise from attributions of social workers' roles from within agency functions, and how social workers might to a greater extent understand some of these particular issues in order to relate to people.

Additional resources

Watch Chris's story in his post on YouTube about how he experienced a psychotic episode, 'Chris talks about his experience of psychosis and his recovery journey' at https://www.youtube.com/watch?v=7BHKV2_wiik, and actor David Harewood's account of his experience of a psychotic episode, 'How psychosis bends your reality – BBC' at https://www.youtube.com/watch?v=MBduR0BU1vg (accessed 17.04.20).

In relation to learning disabilities and behaviour that challenges, see the NICE guideline of 2018 [NG93] (https://www.nice.org.uk/guidance/ng93 (accessed 17.04.20)), which covers services for children, young people and adults with a learning disability, alongside its 2015 guideline, *Challenging behaviour and learning disabilities: prevention and interventions for people with learning disabilities whose behaviour challenges* (https://www.nice.org.uk/guidance/ng11 (accessed 17.04.20)), covering interventions and support for children, young people and adults with a learning disability and behaviour that challenges. These guidelines highlight the importance of understanding the causes of behaviour that challenges, and carrying out thorough assessments so that steps can be taken to help people change their behaviour and improve their quality of life. The guidelines also cover support and intervention for family members or carers.

The 2019 NICE guideline, *Dementia: assessment, management and support for people living with dementia and their carers* [NG97] (https://www.nice.org.uk/guidance/ng97 (accessed 17.04.20)), has useful content on helping with dementia (including Alzheimer's disease), making recommendations on helping carers to support people living with dementia, including working with agitation, aggression and distress (in section 1.7).

Watch the YouTube video produced by staff at University College Los Angeles which includes behavioural challenges for carers in *Managing the late stages of dementia: UCLA Alzheimer's and dementia care* (https://www.youtube.com/watch?v=c5lJqzjce-0n (accessed

17.04.20)), and also a medical doctor's seminar on her knowledge from her professional life and personal experiences on *Dealing with conflict in families living with dementia disabilities* (https://www.youtube.com/watch?v=GmP6g1uUNcg (accessed 17.04.20)).

The NICE (2015b) guidance on *Violence and aggression: short-term management in mental health, health and community settings* (https://www.nice.org.uk/guidance/ng10 (accessed 17.04.20)) provides evidence-based advice on the causes of aggression and violence in mental health work, and ways of assessing and managing risks of conflict in this area for service users, carers and staff.

4 Working with conflict in social work with children, families and young people

In this chapter, we will cover the issues of conflict in terms of the roles social workers play when working with parents and children in safeguarding children work, and in relation to work with looked-after children.

In discussing social workers' roles in child safeguarding work with students and workers in this field, I ask them to think about how they might feel if a social worker came to them saying that they had to enquire about whether their child is being abused. No matter how well social workers introduce themselves – and it is important that we do introduce ourselves and our role in a way which is not judgemental but equally does not avoid the issues of what we have to look into for the sake of the children – I do not think I would normally welcome them and ask them in for a cup of tea in a friendly manner, whether I had been abusing my child or not.

It is acknowledged in the literature that these approaches – as part of the dual role of social work – will inevitably make parents, and very possibly children, concerned about what will happen to them. They will worry about who will tell what to whom, and what the repercussions may be as a result of allegations put to the different family members (and they will almost always be viewed as allegations/accusations by parents), including the children, and what may occur within the family, and to them as a result of the agency's responses, because of this (Hunt et al. 2016).

What then becomes key for work both with parents and with children is that we are as open and honest as we can be about our role, what our concerns might be, in what ways we will discuss with everyone what those concerns are, and how decisions will be made as far as possible between us all – see the hierarchy of engagement table in Chapter 1 – in such scenarios.

In relation to looked-after children, they will very likely have concerns about their sets of relationships with their family of origin, in terms of the role of the local authority and yourself personally in engaging with them, and for their future in terms of education, housing, employment and friendships, as well as later ongoing professional support to aid them with these concerns and worries.

Working with resistant parents in child protection

Social work with children and families has become increasingly dominated by child safeguarding (Parton 2014) and this has resulted in families having more involuntary engagements (when contact has not been sought by the family) with services (Parton 2014).

Reflective exercise: projective understanding

Exercise: In a situation of conflict you are aware of in working with parents in child protection, consider what it is like to be in the position of the worker, the parent(s), and the child.

What might be in the minds of each, and what might they be feeling?

Think through how you are acting in each of the following roles and why, with each setting out how they see the others:

a. For *parents*, fear of the social worker being there only to take their child away; and/or, how/why they may be covering up the abuse of the child? Being unfairly judged, for example because of having mental health problems and/or learning disabilities?
b. For the *worker*, how you might view the parents' and child's motives/actions, and how you would deal with this, and the responses the parents may come up with in 'upping the stakes' if there is resistance?
c. For the *child*, how might they be viewing/experiencing all of this?

This section will examine work with resistant parents in child safeguarding, and how parent service users may respond to the roles staff have to carry out – particularly in terms of the control elements of the work which are needed alongside our supportive and empowering functions. In most work with parents in these situations, social workers do very skilled work, and outcomes are in many situations at least to some extent good for those concerned, in very difficult, challenging and problematic sets of dynamics for the individuals involved. There is, however, a very small minority of parents who are aggressive, resistant and violent in various areas of their lives – towards partners, children, social workers and other health and care staff. Others may have anxieties and feelings of avoidance or aggression, and they may be reacting to the situation due to concerns about them being judged unfairly, e.g. in relation to their learning disability and/or mental health problem, rather than this being a trait within the service user. It may lie on a spectrum of various reasons across these two possibilities.

This small but significantly threatening number of parent/carer service users can attempt to frighten and disempower those in their families – abused children, partners, siblings – and/or informal networks, including the workers. How we come to recognize and respond to such behaviours then becomes an important matter to be dealt with in assessment, staff support, non-abusing family members' support and interventions. The same is true for resistance and disguised compliance (Brandon et al. 2009, 2012; Fauth et al. 2010).

Littlechild et al.'s (2016) survey looked at the experiences of child safeguarding workers in England when working with parents who exhibit aggression and violence. Of the 590 respondents in the survey, 402 were social workers. The behaviours reported included threats, intimidation, abuse, aggravated complaints and physical violence. Some respondents reported that due to the aggression and violence they had faced, they had experienced loss of confidence in carrying out their work. Some workers reported that their ability to protect children had been compromised, with consequent fears of confronting parents appropriately. A number of workers reported significant negative impacts on their own personal health and well-being. Workers expressed concerns about inadequate supervision and support to help them deal with the variety of problems reported in the survey.

Littlechild (2005; Littlechild et al. 2016) found that personalized threats against the worker and their personal networks – 'I know where you live', 'I know where your children go to school', following a social worker in their car – had sometimes produced severe repercussions for workers, and 43 per cent stated that because they did not get enough supervision and support, this led to vulnerable children being put at greater risk when having to deal with hostile and intimidating parents. 26 per cent had received threats to their family, and 67 per cent felt dealing with abusive and hostile parents had led to an impact on their work and family. Workers can be severely affected and become fearful of intervening authoritatively as needed (as opposed to in authoritarian ways).

As one worker said, '*Management do not acknowledge how draining working in hostile situations can be. If you manage the situation and achieve the best outcomes for the child while still maintaining relationships then they tend to just let you get on with it, but this comes at a price for the worker*' (Community Care 2011).

Lord Laming stated in his report for the government on the death of Victoria Climbié that '*Adults who deliberately exploit the vulnerability of children can behave in devious and menacing ways. They will often go to great lengths to hide their activities from those concerned for the well-being of a child . . . [Social work] is a job which carries risks, because in every judgement they make, those staff have to balance the rights of a parent with that of the protection of the child*' (Lord Laming 2003: 13). He suggested social workers needed to practise '*respectful uncertainty*', applying critical evaluation to any information they receive and maintaining an open mind. This becomes a key responsibility for practitioners to take into account in their relationships with parents, and to discuss in supervision. Supervisors also have a responsibility to ensure that practitioners are taking this into account in their work with families, and being supported in dealing with it.

Physical violence

Physical violence and threats can be serious problems in social work, and in child safeguarding work. Physical violence and threats of such violence can often be associated with misuse of various substances, including alcohol. In my own research, and in nationally publicized situations in serious case reviews, physical violence and threats can at times have serious physical and emotional effects, both personally and professionally, on social workers; workers found threats which were personally directed against them as some of the most harrowing

(Hunt et al. 2016; Littlechild et al. 2016). See Chapter 5, which looks at responses to these issues.

Resistance and disguised compliance

Resistance can include disguised compliance, minimal compliance, aggression and violence, which can include verbal abuse and threats, sexual harassment, misogynist abuse, LGBTQ+ abuse, racist abuse and disablist abuse. See Chapter 6 in relation to responding to these types of situations.

Within these challenging situations there can be parental behaviours and challenges on a continuum of types of resistance, from threatened and actual physical violence through to aggravated complaints, avoidance and disguised compliance.

Types, frequency and effects of different forms of aggression, threats, violence, avoidance and resistance

Verbal aggression and threats of violence – frequency and effects

While verbal aggression is known to be quite common, and can be distressing and debilitating over time, it can be that for some people threats of violence are more serious and worrying. As well as actual threats, parents drop you hints about their intimidating behaviours of aggression and violence to social workers in the past, intended to threaten you. They may intimate that they know a lot about your personal life, your family and their movements, and so on. They may follow you in their car. Typically, parents do not do this in front of other professionals, meaning that you are isolated, and there is no evidence to anyone else that it is happening. See also Chapter 6 on abuse and threats over social media and email.

Actual physical violence – frequency and effects

Actual physical violence is rare. It is typified by assaults, and most usually when social workers have to broach that a child protection inquiry is commencing, when parents are told of the decision to take care proceedings, or sometimes in court or immediately afterwards – see Chapter 5 for more on this type of aggression.

Disguised compliance and avoidance – frequency and effects

This kind of behaviour is not uncommon, and is typified by the parent seemingly engaging with the plan for the child, but, for example, in reality they are not attending other agencies as part of the work, typically on issues surrounding drugs work. Some try to 'split' the workers involved by engaging more with one than others, with attempts to engage/collude with one worker by the intimation that they have a special relationship, whereas others are poor workers and/or unhelpful. Parents can also give differential information to different professionals.

They may often avoid appointments, with a variety of reasons given. Among the reasons for these behaviours may be power and control from a very abusive parent to hide the continuing abuse, or, for example, parents with learning disabilities may be fearful of being judged on this and having their children taken away from them.

This is often associated with the 'rule of optimism', in which social workers and other professionals can want to believe the best in the parents, meaning that within strength-based approaches they can lose sight of when parents are not genuinely engaging in becoming safer/more caring/nurturing parents; the parents can be seen as 'playing' the social worker (Dingwall et al. 1983, 2014). The UK government's regulatory *Working Together to Safeguard Children* (HM Government 2018: 28) document states that '*A desire to think the best of adults and to hope they can overcome their difficulties should not subvert the need to protect children from chaotic, abusive and neglectful homes.*'

While violence and threats, and outright refusal is relatively clear, disguised compliance and avoidance is more hidden. Parents may say they agree with the assessment, while in reality they do not – they may attend alcohol/drug misuse support groups because it is part of the plan, but they do not accept the need to change and have no intention of reducing their alcohol/drug intake; they may attend, but are doing this almost mechanically, doing the minimum necessary without any substantial change enacted.

Resistance and aggravated complaints – frequency and effects

This is not uncommon to some degree, and is typified by calling into question the qualifications, actions and the competence of the social worker (Littlechild et al. 2016). It may arise as a result of parents not engaging in meaningful discussion about recognition of concerns or engaging with the agencies in remedying these, and as a way of resisting assessment and intervention, distancing and disempowering the social worker by making aggravated complaints designed to deter the worker from pursuing in an authoritative and appropriate fashion what needs to happen for the safety and well-being of the child. Attempting to undermine the authority of the social worker individually can occur by querying their competence due to age, whether they have children themselves or not, and so on.

Causes of conflict

Exercising authority

When workers have to exercise authority with actively resistant parents they are necessarily challenging the power, authority and control nexus which is often present in that situation. This may escalate parents' strategies to keep the workers at bay. So, if one (or both) of the parents is an abuser, they may use strategies and tactics which they have learned over a long period of time in order to keep other members of the family/network silent about the abuse, with implicit and explicit threats as to what will happen to them if they tell people such as social workers, health workers or education staff what is happening in the family (Goodman-Brown et al. 2003; McElvaney 2003).

As part of our own attributions, if in our work with parents we are frustrated with them about their seeming non-compliance or lack of progress, we may become inappropriately authoritarian, rather than appropriately authoritative. We need to check we are not using distancing and dismissive body language, eye contact, and phrases such as '*this is really unacceptable ... we have spoken about this so many times in the past and we made it clear what needs to happen ... and you are deliberately undermining this*'. The message these words give are from Critical Parent, and communicate that the person is not of worth and is unable to change; it is unlikely we will engage their Adult in this way.

In addition, if a parent has mental health problems, previous experiences of reactions from health and social care staff may mean that they are fearful of what will happen as a result of interventions from social workers in this situation. They may well be concerned that they will be judged unfairly because of the diagnosis they carry, such as personality disorder, schizophrenia, or depression and anxiety. If the parent has some form of learning disability, might this feel the same for them, as it might be for drug misusers? While none of these matters give grounds for not meeting their children's needs as defined in the Children Act 1989, in your assessment of the situation and of why there might be aggressive or resistant behaviours, these parental anxieties need to be appreciated for you to fully understand the reasons for the resistance and then assess and support those parents. This may include problems of how the parents see you in terms of the social work role, and child protection agencies' powers. Understanding this can prepare us to have the open and honest discussions which we emphasize in this book need to take place as far as possible in order to agree how we see each other in our roles and responsibilities. In turn, this allows us to attempt to plan how we will deal with the issues and problems which the agencies might see for the parent(s) in the situation within the hierarchy of engagement set out in Chapter 1.

Cultural relativism versus cultural sensitivity

One key area of conflict which can occur is between social workers of one ethnicity and culture, and parents and families from other ethnic backgrounds and cultures (see, for instance, Healy 2007). As stated in the Social Work England professional standards, social workers must '*Recognise differences across diverse communities and challenge the impact of disadvantage and discrimination on people and their families and communities*'.

At times, social workers can come across as judgemental in relation to their ideas about families from other cultures. But on the other hand, they may not enquire into and pursue assessments and interventions as much as they might, as they may be afraid of being accused of racism. This, then, requires us to be able to confidently carry out work which is culturally sensitive, while at the same time not exhibiting what is being called 'cultural relativism', which can put children at risk (NSPCC 2014). This is where social workers from one particular cultural/ethnic/faith background have little and/or prejudiced knowledge of a particular culture and attribute potentially abusive behaviours to aspects of that culture, which they believe they have no right to 'criticize'. By seeing different cultures in purely relative terms, false assumptions can be made about what is acceptable, and this can place children at risk (Dingwall et al. 1983, 2014; NSPCC 2014). This raises the professional issue of how cultural differences require social workers to appreciate the strengths of different cultural practices, while at the same time having to be aware of the problems involved in cultural relativism.

Key points: the effects of involuntary interventions with parent service users by professionals

- Workers' effectiveness can be compromised when carrying out their roles in supporting families and protecting children
- Effects on professional confidence, and feelings of vulnerability in private life
- Areas of risk are when parents try to keep us at bay, because of their wish for power/control, or maybe concerns about how we will judge the parent more severely because they have mental health problems, learning disabilities, and/or are known drug misusers
- The types of agency responses which professionals experience can be helpful or unhelpful
- Issues of supervision and support from managers are key – social workers need to ensure they receive supervision that provides support in these areas

Ways of dealing with violence, aggression, resistance and disguised compliance

On responding to physical violence, see Chapter 5, and for dealing with abuse, intimidation and harassment of social workers, see Chapter 6. In terms of support that you should demand and expect, see the concluding Chapters 11 and 12.

Reflective exercise: effects of conflictual behaviours

If you have ever been subjected to aggression, violence or threats, or have been involved for example with a colleague who was in this situation, what feelings and thoughts did this evoke for you? Did it affect your confidence in the work with that family, or more generally in your work, and was there any spillover into your personal life?

How do you think this affected your feelings about your work and interventions in that family/other families subsequently?

Reflective exercise: responding to different forms of resistance and aggression

From your consideration of issues for yourself in relation to transactional analysis, the drama triangle and Johari window in Chapter 2, consider how you might respond to the different forms of resistance and aggression, and how you might make use of those tools in thinking about:

1. how your response in a situation could be more effective
2. how you ask for support within your agency to deal with resistance and aggression

The Chief Social Worker for Children (2014: 2) states that social workers should '*Act respectfully even when people are angry, hostile and resistant to change. Manage tensions between parents, carers and family members, in ways that show persistence, determination and professional confidence.*' In addition the Social Work England standards state that social workers must '*Hold different explanations in mind and use evidence to inform my decisions*', which chimes with Lord Laming's idea of respectful uncertainty.

One manager consulted in research in this area stated that important strategies in dealing with challenging service users were (and these are applicable more generally in social work relationships, as referred to in Chapter 2 on generic approaches):

1. To be clear about the role and not 'ducking' this
2. Demonstrating concern for the whole person, if not for parts of their behaviour
3. Giving time to the person and listening respectfully to what they have to say, even if it has to be pointed out that the behaviour is not acceptable (Littlechild 2002)

An important area in terms of responding to such challenging behaviours is to set out clearly and honestly with the parents what your role is, as discussed above. This means setting out clearly the purpose of the assessment or intervention, what the concerns are, and how the engagement with the family will take place and on what basis, with them being able to fully participate in the formulation of what the issues are and how they can be addressed, within the hierarchy of engagement set out in Chapter 1.

Use Adult-to-Adult communication approaches – set out expectations of honesty to and from worker and parents, and ideally record this in the planning/agreement meeting notes, or child protection conference minutes. It is best to try to do this in a way which 'depersonalizes' this approach, so it is clear it is not you personally as an individual making 'criticisms' of the parent.

Consider using approaches such as:

- '*Our areas of concern are . . .*' State clearly, and by doing so depersonalize it from you – '*these are our agency's expectations, so we working with you so we can ensure your child is safe and well*'.
- '*We know it is difficult to be open with us because of your worries about my role/what we are trying/may be planning to do . . .*' Acknowledge your dual role/what your agency's powers are.
- '*Where we need to get to for you and your child is . . . (and why).*' Be specific in relation to well-being/treatment of the child, and in engagement with agencies – and make clear that if your agency is concerned at the parent not engaging, it will need to consider plans again (preferably in an agreement recorded with the parent and other agencies involved).
- '*What needs to change for you and us (agencies) to be assured your child is safe and well?. . . How can that happen?. . . How can we know between us if it is working?*'
- Be persistent in checking out what the parents say about, for example, attending drug misuse agencies, and what they are achieving in them (respectful uncertainty).
- '*Can you tell me your thoughts and feelings on what you learned about . . .?*' (from elements of the agreed plans/interventions).
- '*Can you tell me about what happened . . .? How did you experience . . .? Could you describe what led up to . . .?*'

Make clear to the family that your and other agencies will review these areas over time – with details of when, how, and who will be involved.

In reviewing the progress of the work with the parents, cover:

- '*What changes have you/we seen?*'
- '*What problems have you encountered in trying to change?*'
- '*Who and what has been most helpful to you during this time, and how?*'
- '*Tell me about how your parenting with your child has changed?*'

Reflective exercise: being assertive, not aggressive

How can you be assertive without being aggressive or oppressive, as parents may see it? What might you learn for planning/reviewing such interactions from your consideration of TA, the drama triangle and the Johari window?

Looked-after children

Children who are looked after have often been through traumatic, neglectful and abusive experiences. There is a range of reasons why children and young people enter public care. The child's parents may have agreed to this, or children's services may have intervened for a court to make a legal order. It would be surprising if this did not work its way through into the relationship with the social worker. Further areas that can cause conflict for social workers relate to the high turnover of placements and of social workers, so the young person has often experienced frequent changes of care situation and social worker (Frost 2013), leading to multiplication of issues of problems in attachment learned earlier in their lives, and what is too often a lack of stability for such young people.

In adoption and foster care situations, the young person's learned behaviours can have effects on their TA ego states, as can lack of trust and inner feelings of insecurity and anger from earlier care situations, as well as trauma from abuse and neglect if this was the case, all of which can affect how those children relate to substitute parents. This can lead to strain on siblings in the substitute family, and on those providing the parenting. Again, this can be compounded by a multiple series of placement changes in foster care for them. A high number of looked-after children have had experiences of neglect, abuse, rejection or family breakdown, and so such change of care situations will not aid their building of trust and feeling confident to build attachments. The effects of all this can be '*complex and life-long, influencing emotional and physical wellbeing, social and educational opportunity, effective self-sufficiency, personal relationships and resilience*' (Rees 2006: 83).

In terms of residential young people's units, the issues of staff, however committed, coming on and off shift, with staff leaving and new ones arriving, mixed with the dynamics within residential young people's units, are important factors. Experience of changes in terms of individuals regularly coming and going, both staff and other young people, are destabilizing factors, all of which can influence the young person's feelings and expression of emotions, sometimes including aggression. This may well make the young person feel excluded and insecure, particularly where bullying may occur (Barter et al. 2004).

So there could be real concerns and possibly resentments from the young person about the reasons for this 'removal'. Did their parents not love them enough to keep them? Have their parents been judged by social workers to not be good enough to take care of them? There are likely to be mixed feelings for a child or young person in these types of situations, and social workers need to have an empathetic projective understanding of the types of issues that might lead to such concerns and resentment, with perhaps a dismissive or aggressive attitude towards social workers, possibly with anti-authority feelings, alongside a sense of abandonment.

It must be noted that many young people who are looked after do not have these feelings or behaviours to any significant degree, if at all. Most children in care say that their experiences are good, and that it was the right choice for them (Biehal et al. 2014).

However, negative feelings as set out above are the reality for many young people, and it is the duty of social workers to try to understand and relate to these feelings, even when it can feel that the resentment and disengagement by the young person is very alienating.

Responding to young people's needs

Cree and Davis's research with service users with experience of a wide range of services found that their expectations were of '*responsiveness, building relationships, being person centred, providing emotional and practical support, being holistic, balancing rights, risks and protection, being evidence based, future oriented and there for the long term*' (Cree and Davis 2007: 149). These findings resonate with the areas of importance for other service user groups covered in this book, in relation to the types of approaches and the ways of discussing issues with service users and carers in order to avoid conflict building up from what in many situations has the inherent potential to lead to conflict. Social workers need to use their knowledge and skills to recognize what may be happening with the service user /carer, and openly recognize and discuss this in a non-judgemental/non-provocative way.

Conclusion

This chapter has covered how parents and children may be experiencing the safeguarding process, how looked-after children may experience their situation, and how this might frame the way they approach you in your social work role. It has examined the possible conflicts arising from the vulnerabilities and types of resistance some people may have in these situations, and how it is important to be clear about the possibilities and limitations of the social work role. It has looked at how social workers need to try to appreciate what they bring to the work in these areas in addition to what the service users may be bringing, and how to consider this within the conflicts that may arise in these roles.

Additional resources

HM government's (2018) *Working Together to Safeguard Children: A Guide to Inter-Agency Working to Safeguard and Promote the Welfare of Children* is an important document and set of principles and procedures, as it is the regulatory document concerning how all professionals in all agencies working with children should approach parents, children and other professionals where safeguarding is an issue: https://assets.publishing.service.gov.uk/government/uploads/system/uploads/attachment_data/file/779401/Working_Together_to_Safeguard-Children.pdf (accessed 17.04.20).

Department for Education's (2018a) *Information sharing advice for safeguarding practitioners: Guidance on information sharing for people who provide safeguarding services to children, young people, parents and carers* from the Department for Education is again an important document for all professionals to be aware of with regard to sharing of information between agencies: https://www.gov.uk/government/publications/safeguarding-practitioners-information-sharing-advice (accessed 17.04.20).

5 Dealing with physical violence and threats from service users and carers: personal approaches and organization responsibilities

This chapter addresses how social workers, their managers and agencies can best assess conflict concerning risks in dealing with physical violence and threats from service users and carers. This will include recognition of risks to yourself, and what to do about this in ensuring agency support. In face-to-face situations, the chapter will include personal strategies of both non-verbal and verbal communication techniques and ways of defusing situations, as well as agency strategies.

It aims to set out for managers and front-line staff how to assess risks of the different forms of physical violence and threats, alongside an understanding of the effects on yourself, and on the service user. These areas cross over with issues of other types of abuse and harassment that social workers can experience from service users, which are covered in Chapter 6.

Key points for social workers and their managers

For social workers: Effects of the different forms of aggression and violence can be both professional and personal, and affect the work you do.

You need to be aware of your own responses to assessing such risks and as Social Work England makes clear, '*Report . . . any dangerous, abusive or discriminatory behaviour or practice*' and consequently ensure you ask for support from your employers in such scenarios.

For managers: Social workers need to be supported proactively in terms of risk assessment, and supported in the planning for their work. Supervisors and managers need to ensure they have plans to support staff, taking into account the knowledge of effects on staff's practice, well-being and personal support networks.

Defining violence

Skills for Care's (undated b: 3) guide for employers refers to the Health and Safety Executive (HSE) definition of work-related violence as '*Any incident in which a person is abused, threatened or assaulted in circumstances relating to their work. This includes sexual and racial harassment, and threats to family and property.*'

The guide states that employers are responsible for setting out the organization's policy and arrangements for managing the risks arising from violence and aggression, and for having clear procedures explaining the risk assessment process, including initial assessment of the individual and family. Workers, it states, should be fully involved in this process, so staff will know what to do when there is thought to be a risk or if an encounter is escalating into a possible violent incident. It also expects agency provision/communications to be clear about appropriate and timely support after an incident (including out of hours if required) to help the victim recover from the experience, and in taking action against the perpetrator. This chapter will look at how we can best make use of this guidance.

The nature and extent of physical violence and threats

Violence, aggression and difficult behaviours towards staff are a significant problem in social work and social care (BASW 2018b). The employers' organization Skills for Care's (2013) research report on violence against social care workers demonstrated that violence and abuse has a negative impact on staff morale, motivations, retention, absenteeism, perception of staff value and stress levels in the workplace.

Violence and threats from service users can significantly affect workers' capacity to carry out their work effectively, and their commitment to that work (Denney 2010; Littlechild et al. 2016), although the effects of this on social workers' practice and personal lives are frequently ignored in the literature (Littlechild 2005; Community Care 2010, 2014).

In 2010, a Community Care (2010) survey found that nine out of ten social workers had suffered abuse, assaults and threats, being punched, stabbed, strangled, kicked and assaulted.

The effects are not only professional, but also affect workers' private lives – close friends, partners and immediate family in particular may suffer from the demands placed in this way on those employed in social work posts – which are often stressful already (Cooper 2011). Workers have paid for their vocation with serious injury, emotional trauma and even sometimes, though thankfully very rarely, their lives. This is a commitment that is perhaps too rarely acknowledged in the media or by politicians, for those who regularly take on these risks. Social workers knock on doors and enter situations where risks are present, and will attempt to manage those risks so that service users and the wider public remain safe and well. They enter into or work in residential and day care situations where they know there are service users who are likely be aggressive and abusive. Social workers' commitment to their helping role is a strength but also a potential area of risk, in terms of how we may need to more often balance risks to ourselves while giving the best service to service users and carers.

Some examples of types of violence and aggression:

- Someone who has a long history of mental distress and intervention from mental health agencies, with experience of coercive measures from social workers, for example in the Approved Mental Health Practitioner role, scared about seeing a social worker and what might happen as a result of this, starting to become aggressive and threatening.
- The adult receiving day services, who has learning disabilities to the extent that they can feel threatened by staff approaches, and reacts aggressively.
- The person with severe dementia who, on each visit, thinks her home carer is a stranger, sees her as a threat and a thief, and strikes out 'in defence' of herself and her property.
- The young person who is looked after in public care, who has had models of aggression and violence in their background, and who may be feeling bereft in terms of family support and potential for the future, who was hoping to see members of their family of origin at the weekend, but gets a message on the Friday evening that they have pulled out of this, and they become aggressive and challenging.

Recognizing and working with our own personal issues

In order to reduce the risk of violence and aggression, we need to examine our own ways of reacting to the different types of such situations, and ways of coping with them, to see if these are the best responses to these problems as presented in our working lives, as in the exercise below.

Reflective exercise: preparing yourself for possible violence

Social workers:

- What could alert you to possible risk of aggression before you see the service user(s)?
- How can we best recognize warning signs that service users/carers might present us with, in the immediate situation we are in, but also in how this might alert us to the need to get support from colleagues/managers, and how best to ensure we get that support from them?
- Do we ever think we may not have recognized a potentially violent situation when we might have done? Why might that have been? Might that help us to be more aware of risks?

Managers:

- This element of recognition of warning signs overlaps with organizational responses over the issue of how much emphasis is given by managers/employers to identifying potentially violent situations.
- How can managers best ensure they and social workers recognize and ask for appropriate support when necessary?

Personal approaches where there is possible violence and aggression

Practical considerations

In the following sections, we will consider practical responses within this framework to make yourself feel, and be, more secure in your work.

Practical strategies will depend partly on the nature of the threat. Is it a physical threat? Or is it abuse, bullying, racist, etc.? If so, see Chapter 6. And in any of these situations, how do you recognize it is a threat? Do you maybe (erroneously) believe this is what you have to put up with in your type of work? You might be worried you will be seen as making a 'fuss over nothing', or as a demanding 'troublemaker'. How you frame – and change – your own internal thinking and 'self-talk' on these issues will affect your confidence and assertiveness. The use of transactional analysis (TA) and the Johari window are then useful tools to enable you to feel more confident about risk, knowing what you need, and what you have a right to. This is nested within knowledge of agency policy and procedures, and the legal and regulatory framework, as set out in Chapter 11.

Assessing risk

Preparation checklist: risk assessment

- Check if there have been any problems in this way with the service user(s) before – as a general point, if someone has done something or behaved in a certain way before, they are more likely to do so again, in similar circumstances.
- If you judge that there is a risk from this, ensure you take risk management measures and record these and your communications about this with your managers.
- Where at all possible, take time to think through the situation with your manager and/or colleagues when you have identified the possibility of the threat of violence. Check what support is available in the situation you are in/about to be in, based on that assessment of risk.
- Work out an exit strategy for you and others who may be at risk.
- Anticipate any equipment you may need, such as a mobile phone, attack alarm or sim card alert. Do not rely exclusively on these, however, as they are only additional preventive and protective measures to be applied as part of the risk assessment process.

- Expect the unexpected: your employer should have procedures that staff follow in the event of an unpredictable or unexpected incident. Your employer should tell you about these procedures and you should familiarize yourself with them and remind yourself of them from time to time.

Key points on assessing risk

Skills for Care's guide on combating violence against care staff sets out advice on this as follows:

> *When you think there is a risk, discuss your concerns with colleagues and managers*
>
> *Use local systems to check whether other professionals have flagged concerns*
>
> *Gather as much information as possible about people who use services where violence is threatened*
>
> *Share information about potentially violent users of services with colleagues, your manager, other departments and other organisations*
>
> (Skills for Care undated b: 2:5).

Consider where you will see the person; will it be best to invite them to your office, to be on your territory, for example, or elsewhere? Make sure you appraise yourself of relevant procedures and policies, and engage others in plans to support you – particularly if you are to go on a visit away from your base, where you are at most risk of serious harm.

Is there prominent contextual recording of previous incidents or information from other agencies on files/computer records for reference for you and others as part of your risk assessments?

Social work staff who work in community settings should be provided with personal safety alarms or smartphones and apps for lone worker safety. Check and make use of your agency's lone worker policies if that may be an issue. Do people know where you are and what to do if you do not contact them by a certain time?

Be aware of any drugs (legal or illegal), including alcohol, that the service user may have taken or be taking. The more they have taken, the less a reasoning and reasonable approach will be effective.

It is important to ensure you are not making decisions about risk on your own, or taking risky actions on your own. This is not being demanding or awkward – you should do this for your own safety and well-being, as you are required to do under legislation (Health and Safety at Work Act 1974); while your employer has a duty to support you in these ways under that legislation, it also requires you personally not to put yourself in situations of risk.

Different settings

Office interviews

In an office situation, arrange for a colleague/manager to telephone in after five or ten minutes, so they can check if you need assistance. Agree what each of you will say to alert them you need them to come in, on some pretext maybe (for example, there is a call from the chief executive/director that you have to take urgently), and if this does not work, a way to get you out/protected, and then be with colleagues to plan the next move. So, consider possible psychological strategies/escape routes, as well as physical tactics and strategies. Such back-up may include having someone wait outside the door; the door should have a means of surveillance from other staff such as being partly glazed, and if not it should perhaps be left partly open. Prepare clearly what action will be taken on your behalf by colleagues in a given situation.

If you are to be alone with a potentially violent service user, consider taking a colleague into the interview with you. If you do this, have a good rationale for their presence that you can tell to the service user, as otherwise it may give them the message that you are worried by them/distrustful of them, which will not help the situation. Agree what role each of you will take, the aims of the session, and how/when it will finish.

Home visits

If you see the service user(s) in their home – as is the case in many child safeguarding and mental health situations – how can you ensure you have supportive surveillance from colleagues/managers? Do you have a mobile phone that can be used at the press of a button to alert agencies to support you, with a GPS system linked to a security agency? Arrange for a colleague to call you after a certain period if you have not returned, considering the same issues as in the section above about office interviews. Where there is a risk to staff safety, employers should ensure social workers are enabled to undertake home visits in pairs or facilitate office-based contact with service users.

Day/residential settings

If the venue is a day/residential setting, consider whether it is best to see the person in an office space, or in their territory. Either way, consider that if a conflict situation develops, it is not in front of an audience of other service users, as this can exacerbate the situation; it is difficult for people to back down from confrontation in such circumstances.

Reflective exercise: preparing yourself personally for possible violence

1. How can you use your reflection about your ways of using your thinking concerning your Parent/Adult/Child ego states (Chapter 2) in terms of your

previously learned ways of reacting, to update your ways of recognizing, planning and responding to the different types of violent, aggressive and uncooperative behaviours?
2. What might you consider may be new ways for you to think about for your personal strategies/tactics for defusing potential violence?
3. How might you come across to service users/carers in relation to different types of these situations, from your consideration of projective understanding, the drama triangle and the Johari window?

Face-to-face situations

If you find yourself in a situation where violence becomes an immediate possibility, you need to have a brief checklist you can remember and apply from your consideration of your own personal responses, but also including how you plan to call for help, within agency policies.

Reflective exercise: what could alert you to possible risk of escalating aggression

What could alert you to the risk of escalating aggression during your face-to-face contact?

1. What in the service user's body language/eye contact/physical and defensible space/use of voice/words and tone and volume being used could be noticed?
2. How are they relating to you, and perceiving your attitudes, motives, role, and your use of body language/eye contact/physical and defensible space/use of voice/words and tone and volume?
3. What are the best ways you can use your skills and knowledge to de-escalate any rising aggression?
4. If you are there with a manager/colleague, have you discussed how you will react if the service user starts to be aggressive or violent? How will you support each other, and in what ways?

In terms of physical space actions, it is best to sit down if possible, at the same level as the service user. You are then in a less aggressive stance. Try to maintain a relaxed-looking posture. 'Squaring up' to the service user is rarely helpful. Sitting or standing at a 45° angle is much better than being face to face.

Do try your best to stay aware of your own feelings, and your reactions to those of your service user; you are then more able to adjust your responses and therefore reduce the risk of violence.

What might you be doing to exacerbate things if you sense that the situation is escalating? Try to see/listen how you may be coming across to them – might differences in ethnicity be affecting how you might inadvertently be coming across as unfairly 'judging' the person, or as oppressive? The same issues arise for gender differences, and where the service user has mental health problems, certain types and levels of learning disabilities, and/or drug misuse problems. In my own personal background, with the best will in the world, my Parent state may have messages about for example BAME groups and/or immigrants, which in my Adult I find objectionable and reject. However, given our knowledge of how such issues may affect us, I may not be aware of these as much as I would like because of areas I do not recognize – as set out in the Johari window – where I am being prejudicial in some way, which might take me into one of the positions in the drama triangle. I might, for example, inadvertently start becoming a Persecutor and making someone else the Victim, because of these unacknowledged issues.

Do try to be aware of putting across and making it clear to the service user that you are doing your best to listen to – if not necessarily agreeing with or condoning – what they are saying, and communicate that you have heard them. Recognizing and affirming that you understand the service user's thoughts and feelings is important, as is communicating that recognition to them.

Try not to:

- Get into a verbal battle or feel or act as if you always have to win a point if it seems something is intractable between you and an aggressive service user, who is becoming more and more aggressive.
- Get locked into repetitive verbal exchanges – say things in different ways. However, sometimes repeating a phrase authoritatively but uncritically can calm someone down.
- Start to become defensive, and become aggressive yourself towards the service user who is being aggressive to you. This may be something you need to possibly unlearn from models or parental messages in your past, or what you have learned for example as an adolescent in groups.
- Put yourself or the service user, either physically or psychologically, in a corner. If on your own premises, make sure the room you will use is set out to allow both yourself and the other person to have an escape route if they are feeling angry, so they can leave without having to negotiate with you to get past you or any other obstacle. Make sure if you can that you each have exits and that either of you can back away without 'losing face'.
- Show that you are afraid, or get into an aggressive mode in trying to conceal your fear/anxiety. Hear your own voice; modulate it and try to keep it firm but calm. Use eye contact, but don't stare. Too forceful eye contact can appear threatening and increase your service user's hostility. In particular, be very careful of your use of eye contact with people who are in a psychotic state. Also, use of appropriate eye contact varies greatly across cultures and gendered areas, and so it is important you become aware of this in terms of cultural sensitivity.

- Touch someone who is in a psychotic state. They may well be feeling vulnerable, and believe you are misleading them or putting them in danger of some sort – the person may believe, absolutely sincerely, that you are about to violate them in some way, and try to protect themselves violently.

Touching is a debatable point in social work, and very much so in residential work. In the right circumstances, touching someone on the arm or shoulder could be a way of showing that you are concerned and want to help them calm down. However, depending on the state the other person is in and what attributions they have towards you, this may be the trigger for them to be violent towards you. In addition, you need to be aware in terms of cultural sensitivity what touch can mean in different circumstances across different ethnic and cultural groups – for example, from issues of gender, for you to be aware of how close in terms of physical proximity you should be in respecting others' ethnic and cultural sensitivities.

If matters are getting out of hand, try to depersonalize the conflict between yourself and the service user and/or carer, and move it back into the domain of agency situations and roles – acknowledge this with the service user, in that the interaction between you is not resolving the issues. Try to suggest or make arrangements to meet another time, possibly with a colleague or manager, or agree to let them discuss the problematic matters with you and/or your manager as soon as possible. This could become a form of dispute resolution or service mediation – see Chapter 11. This also gives you time to put supports in place for your next meeting, or in discussion with your manager you may decide a further meeting with the service user/carer, either on your own or with others, would be too risky for you. If it will be too difficult for you to appropriately meet the service user and/or challenge what is happening in the situation with them, work out another strategy with other staff/managers to deal with this in a more effective way. Where the service user has become too alienated from you to be able to work towards something more positive, this needs to be worked on and decided on in supervision/planning meetings.

Where possible, try not to constrict the service user's physical space. Allow room for movement. Being physically overbearing can increase the service user's anxiety, vulnerability and/or anger at their lives being controlled, and their consequent hostility. This point can be taken literally or figuratively, as in psychological space and room for movement.

If necessary, try to remove yourself and the service user from a group if the group presence is exacerbating things, and if you think you will be safer with them on their own. It can be harder to back down in front of peers in a group for both the worker and the service user.

It is important to consider removing yourself if it becomes obvious the service user is rapidly becoming more aggressive or is about to attack you. If you feel you need to leave, you might consider leaving the room if you are in your own setting, but give a reason for this – for instance, say you will go to check an issue out for them, or you need to talk to someone else, anything that is feasible and believable – and this will give you a chance to organize appropriate support and back-up. Say where you are going, and what you are going to do – economy with the truth may be valuable here – and how long you will be. This can also allow a little cooling off time for you both, and relief from the 'squaring up' to each other situation which can escalate the situation rather than calm it down.

As a way of giving other options rather than the focus being on you, you might try to arrange to give the person advice about going to the complaints procedure and/or your manager, and how they can access this easily, so they feel they have a route for their anger/grievance to be dealt with. This may help to take it away from them seeing you as an individual who is disbelieving them/being disrespectful/using your power unfairly over them. In the author's safeguarding children research mentioned in Chapter 4, some of the most severe effects on workers were when the service user personalized the aggression against the worker individually rather than focusing this on the agency.

Consider calling the police if there is physical violence against yourself or a colleague, if you are able to do this, or immediately after an event if you have managed to get yourself out of it, with or without the support of colleagues or managers. This is partly because it is important to inform the police of such violent acts, but also in case, as has happened on a number of occasions, the service user has returned with the intention of carrying out further violent acts, or following the worker outside the office on foot/in their car, to threaten them further. Some service users have targeted car parks where workers park their cars – ensure you are safe when you leave the premises if there has been a violent incident.

What to do after an event: checklist

Engage a supporter in the work setting to think through or plan how you can be protected from further harassment or assault. For example, is there a possibility that an assailant will try to come back in the immediate future to do it again? Are doors and windows secured against this? Do the police need to be informed, if they have not been already? Do you need protection in making your way home?

- Do obtain support and consultation afterwards – check what your employing agency has in place for such services through your manager or human resources department.
- Do discuss with your managers and colleagues any issues that could have helped prevent the violence.
- Do consider completing prominent contextual recording on files for reference for others as part of risk assessments in the future. Aim to record fully the reasons you can identify for the violence or aggression, ideally in a debriefing session after the event, possibly in the form of a critical incident analysis (see Chapter 11 on this). As part of such a debriefing, in discussing what was important in the build-up to and the triggers for the violence, try to identify ways the same sort of situation could be dealt with differently in the future, and place this prominently on the service user's file/computer record. Where at all possible, you should agree the content of this with them if it is safe to do so, taking account of the hierarchy of engagement set out in Chapter 1, as this can

be important as a way of giving limits and boundaries to service users' behaviour. In addition, it allows their perspective to be recorded as well.

Issues for responding to the service user/carer

It is important to take up the matter with managers, to ensure you are supported properly, but also to ensure the issues for the service user and/or carer are considered. How we do this is important: ensuring that while we make clear we are accepting the person, and value them as a human being, we have to work with them on how that behaviour is not acceptable, and on how this can be dealt with between yourself and them. If the event was very serious, do consider prosecution with the support of your employer, and/or an order to protect you under the Protection from Harassment Act. In addition, consider with your manager if you should continue to work with the service user, and if so on what basis, and with what messages and limit and boundary setting with the service user from your manager/agency. See Chapter 11 for more detail on these areas.

From the manager or supporter's point of view, following up such support is also important, so that the promised phone call that night to the victim is made, and that in subsequent days the supporter(s) asks in an unobtrusive way how the victim is. The need to be sensitively cared for, and to feel that this is happening, is an important feature in someone regaining their equilibrium, particularly in the workplace, where we know victims are keenly aware and concerned about the reactions of colleagues (Littlechild 1997).

Key points: immediate effects on the victim

Bursting into tears

Statements such as '*I'm OK really, I'll carry on – anyway, I have to see a service user in 20 minutes. I'll be OK*', while they look and sound shaken and disorientated – it is likely that someone in such a state should not be allowed just to carry on as usual, for their own sake, but also for the service users they will see and the other work they might be doing, which may well be negatively affected by their emotional reactions.

'*I'm scared of leaving the office. What if they are still there, waiting for me, or follow my car?*'

'*They have said they know where I live, and where my children go to school . . .*'

'*They were telling me in a really menacing way how their brother who they are very close to had been in jail for assaulting police officers and social workers . . .*'

'*I don't think I can work with them anymore, I am too scared.*'

'*How dare they . . . I am going to get them back* [or similar phrase] *for that.*'

'*I'm going to see to it that they are made to know they can't do this sort of thing.*'

'*What happens when I see them next?*'

Reflective exercise for managers

- Would you feel comfortable as a manager or a colleague in supporting someone who is experiencing such emotions/reactions? If not, why not? How could you better prepare yourself to do this?
- How could you best support your worker:

  i. in the immediate situation?
  ii. that evening?
  iii. next day?
  iv. following up days later – and possibly even longer term than this?

Longer term effects

A few days, or perhaps several weeks after the incident, the victim can seem less their normal self, and may be quieter and less confident, or more angry and uptight. They hesitate in facing situations they have never been reticent about before, especially situations which might mean them confronting or challenging, going into new situations, or into similar ones to the incident(s) that affected them (Littlechild 1997).

Conclusion

This chapter has set out the types of situations in which physical violence might become a possibility, and how you can consider using risk assessments in trying to prevent them happening. It has looked at how you might think about preventing exacerbation of the potential for aggression and violence in a situation, from your thinking about ideas from transactional analysis. This includes how you might be able to modify how you are coming over in order to modify the behaviour of yourself, as well as that of the service user or carer. The effects of such physical violence have been examined, with discussion of how immediate and longer term effects on the social worker need to be taken into account, in terms of victims' needs, and protection from possible further violence.

Additional resources

The Skills for Care guidance, *Work Smart, Work Safe: Combating Violence Against Care Staff*, available online at https://www.skillsforcare.org.uk/Document-library/Standards/Safety-guidance/Work-smart,-work-safe—guide-for-employees.pdf (accessed 17.04.20), provides very useful guidance to employees on employers' responsibilities, your own responsibilities, assessing risk and planning ahead, steps to take after an incident, and support you should expect.

Skills for Care's two published research reports in 2013 address the prevalence of violence against social work and social care staff, and ways that are or can be used in organizations for dealing with this violence. They set out the negative impact on staff morale, motivation, retention, absenteeism, perception of staff value and stress levels in the workplace. See *Violence Against Social Care and Support Staff: Summary of Research*, available at: https://www.skillsforcare.org.uk/Document-library/NMDS-SC,-workforce-intelligence-and-innovation/Research/Violence-reports/Violence-against-social-care-workers—composite-report.pdf (accessed 24.04.20), and the Institute of Public Care/Skills for Care (2013) *Violence Against Social Care and Support Staff: Evidence Review*, available at: https://www.skillsforcare.org.uk/Document-library/NMDS-SC,-workforce-intelligence-and-innovation/Research/Violence-reports/Violence-against-social-care-workers—evidence-review.pdf (accessed 24.04.20).

6 Dealing with abuse and harassment from service users and carers

This chapter covers areas of non-physical violence and threats, including abusive behaviour, bullying, sexual/racist/disablist/LGBTQ+ abuse, and harassment against social work staff.

The nature of social work practice, and the dual role which social workers have, balancing out the rights and interests of different people involved in situations, can mean that social workers are often open to abuse and harassment from service users and carers. These types of behaviours from colleagues, managers and staff from other agencies is dealt with in Chapter 9. While we need to acknowledge that there are situations where social workers have abused their power over service users and carers, this book examines an area which is not often a feature of social work education and training – how some service users and carers can bully and harass social workers, and the effects this has.

The employers' organization Skills for Care in its 2013 report on violence (Skills for Care 2013) indicated that violence and abuse has a negative impact on staff morale, motivation, retention, absenteeism, perception of staff value and stress levels in the workplace.

The chapter takes you through what the different types of abuse and harassment might be, and ideas on how best to try to deal with it.

Bullying

There is no simple definition of bullying as it can take many different forms, but it is usually seen as persistent offensive, intimidating, humiliating behaviour, which attempts to undermine an individual or group of people. Bullying is generally carried out face to face but can also occur in writing, by telephone, text messaging, email and on social media. Usually if a person genuinely feels they are being singled out for unfair treatment they may well be experiencing bullying, with an issue that needs to be addressed.

Bullying is not completely divorced from harassment – harassment can be seen as part of bullying, but the term harassment and its nature is defined legally, whereas bullying is not.

Some of the ideas as to why this may happen in individual situations, from service users, include:

- feelings from service users and carers of being oppressed by the social worker's role, for example because of their ethnicity

- service users' feelings of being disempowered/oppressed when they need support, but where the social worker is unable to provide this, because of decisions in the agency based on eligibility criteria, and the social worker is the person relaying this news
- ways of trying to keep social workers from being involved in the situation, particularly in relation to where feelings of the service user's personal rights and interests are being challenged, for example where there is someone who may be abusing a vulnerable adult or a child
- learned behaviour in some service users and carers about acting this way in order to have power and control over others, often in situations where some people wish to take/maintain power and control in domestic situations over partners, family, etc.

In responding to such abuse, social workers first need to recognize that it is happening. This might not be so easy, and relates back to the ideas raised in Chapter 2 concerning transactional analysis and the three ego states, where our learned and modelled experiences from our learning as a child can affect our ability to engage our Adult. This lays the foundation within us about what we need to be aware of in order to ensure that we can recognize when we are in a Parent or Child state, which may affect our experiences of, and reactions to, behaviours from service users and carers. All or any of the forms of abuse or harassment may then buy into and affect your being in one of your Critical Parent or Adapted Child ego states.

So, for example, if I come from a family or culture in which abuse and threats are accepted or even condoned, this may affect my experiences of working with parents – so it may be that I am caught in my Adapted Child rather than my Adult, where I react in ways similar to how I felt when I was disempowered and maybe felt fearful in relation to those forms of abuse, aggression and control.

These neglected areas of theory and practice in social care and social work – how your own reactions as a human being may affect your practice, and the effective recognition and responses to threatening situations in our work – mean that it is valuable, when necessary, to raise these issues in your supervision, and try to unravel them. It can be useful to consider your responses as part of your reflective practice, including how you do this from an understanding of transactional analysis, the drama triangle and the Johari window. This may help to better understand why service users and carers may exhibit fearful, aggressive and conflict-laden behaviours, but also for you to understand yourself and your reactions in the same way. By engaging your Adult ego state effectively, this can help you to recognize these feelings in yourself and your Parent and 'childlike' ego states, and review and critically analyse the learning you may have had from parental figures in your own childhood that can distort behaviours/interactions with others.

Protection from abuse and harassment

The Equality Act 2010 gives certain groups of people protection from discrimination and harassment in the workplace and in wider society.

The Equality Act sets out the basic framework of protection against direct and indirect discrimination, harassment and victimization in services and public functions, providing protection for people discriminated against because they are perceived to have, or are associated with someone who has, a protected characteristic (Government Equalities Office 2010).

Aggressive and threatening behaviour can include abusive behaviour, threats, sexual, racist, disablist, homophobic/biphobic/transphobic abuse, bullying and harassment. These are sometimes presented in conjunction with threats of physical violence (this is dealt with in Chapter 5). In bullying and harassment, a key issue is that the person carrying out the bullying and harassment, of varying forms, is attempting to produce fear in the victim and keep them from telling others or gaining support from them.

The British Association of Social Workers survey

In a survey of social workers carried out in Northern Ireland in 2018, the British Association of Social Workers (BASW) Northern Ireland branch found that abuse, intimidation, threats and violence to social workers were common among the 270 respondents (BASW 2018a).

In fact, 86 per cent of social workers in the survey had experienced intimidation intended to make them worried or afraid; 75 per cent had received threats, and 50 per cent had been subjected to physical violence. Some had been prevented from leaving the service user's home. The intimidating behaviour reported included overt as well as subtle means to undermine and discredit social workers, as well as thinly veiled threats to cause harm to them and/or their families. There were instances of verbal abuse, swearing, name calling and sectarian or racist abuse. Experience of severe verbal abuse left them feeling '*mentally battered*' or '*harangued*' (BASW 2018a: 7), and '*It wasn't so much being threatened by the young person, it was in fact the relentless abuse of myself and my colleagues, on a daily basis, that was difficult to deal with*' (Residential Childcare Social Worker) (BASW 2018a: 7).

A significant number of the threats included a paramilitary link, a particular issue for Northern Ireland. Forty per cent said they had been in an organization, in a team, or had a colleague that had been subjected to a threat by a criminal or paramilitary group.

Another issue frequently cited as problematic by respondents was the use of complaints processes to intimidate them. Various examples were provided of vexatious complaints made, usually to the professional registration body, but also to employers, elected representatives and the police, and these formed a key factor in undermining social workers' confidence in carrying out their work. In Littlechild et al.'s research (2016), 77 per cent of respondents had been threatened with complaints. While the majority of these will at least in part be justified, some are clearly meant to threaten and distance the worker. See Chapter 4 for more on this in the child safeguarding arena.

In the Northern Ireland BASW survey, implied threats were used when service users set out to social workers personal information about them – their home address, car registration number, or knowledge about the schools their children attended. Respondents recounted how service users waited outside their offices, and how they or their family members had been followed in their cars – behaviours also found in earlier research (Littlechild 2005; Littlechild et al. 2016). At the most severe end, respondents had received death threats, threats of rape and threats of torture.

Key points: assessing risk in relation to abuse and harassment

The various types of bullying and harassment can greatly affect the practice of social workers, and their safety and well-being. You need to be aware of when you may be about to enter into such a situation, and consider how you will gain support from your employer in relation to this, which they are legally bound to provide.

In terms of carrying out an assessment of the risks of abuse and harassment, it is important for you and your employer to check any indicators of such previous behaviours from colleagues and records in your agency, but also from other agencies.

Harassment

Harassment is a legal term for unwanted behaviour that you find offensive, where the other person's behaviour is because:

- you have a protected characteristic
- there is any connection with a protected characteristic (for example, you are treated as though you have a particular characteristic, even if the other person knows this isn't true)

Harassment that is based on a person's protected characteristic – sex, race, religion or belief, sexual orientation, disability, gender reassignment, pregnancy, marriage and civil partnership status and/or age – is in breach of the Equality Act 2010. Workplace harassment has a specific definition under the Equality Act 2010, when someone's behaviour is meant to have, or has, the effect of either violating someone's dignity, or creating an intimidating, hostile, degrading, humiliating or offensive environment for them.

Unwanted behaviour could include:

- spoken or written abuse
- offensive emails
- tweets or comments on websites and social media
- images and graffiti
- physical gestures
- facial expressions
- banter that is offensive to you (see https://www.equalityhumanrights.com/en/advice-and-guidance/what-harassment-and-victimisation)

Harassment and abuse can range from ill-considered remarks not intended to be hurtful, through to deliberate physical attacks that cause serious injury. Harassing abuse, bullying and violence can be identified by the motivation of the bully, the language used, and/or by the fact that victims are singled out because of, for example in racism, the colour of someone's skin, the way they talk, their ethnic grouping or by their religious or cultural practices.

In relation to issues of race discrimination and race hate, fair treatment is a legal duty. Employers have a responsibility to investigate and respond to any such issue they become aware of. They also have to take all reasonable measures to protect employees from harassment if a service user or carer abuses an employee in such ways.

Cyberbullying

One growing form of abuse and harassment of social workers is in relation to the increased use of social media, which has been seen in particular in relation to safeguarding children work and adoption work.

Little research has been done on this area to date. Kagan et al. (2017) found that the issue of service users' misuse of electronic technologies against social workers was becoming a problem in Israel, with cyberbullying becoming a new form of bullying in addition to the more traditional forms. Respondents in the BASW research (2018a) had experienced a growth in social media abuse, for example where service users or their family members were spreading false and malicious information about social workers via Facebook and YouTube, and it was playing a role in enabling threats against social workers. Eleven per cent of respondents had received a threat over social media, and 4 per cent had a family member who had been threatened in this way. Staff experiencing threats through social media found them particularly worrying.

Third-party bullying and harassment

A 'third party' refers to '*someone who a worker interacts with as part of their job but who is not employed by the same employer as them*' (TUC 2019a).

A recent Trades Union Congress (TUC) poll (TUC 2019a) found that at least half of young workers had been subjected to third-party abuse and harassment behaviour three or more times. Nearly two-thirds had experienced verbal abuse from a third party in the previous year. Nearly two in five of workers who had experienced third-party abuse and harassment were less confident at work as a result, and nearly one in four said it had a negative impact on their performance at work. More than one in three reported a negative impact on their mental health, by feeling more stressed, anxious and/or depressed, while 22 per cent said it had made them want to leave their job. Less than half of the respondents who had experienced this had reported the most recent incident to their employer.

The TUC (2019a) maintains that the Health and Safety at Work Act 1974 states that employers have a duty to ensure the health, safety and welfare of their employees. This includes preventing abuse, harassment and bullying; an employer should act to protect a member of staff who is being abused or harassed by a third party, in the same way as if they were being harassed by a colleague (TUC 2019a). Workers or students who are harassed by a third party can claim support from their employing agencies/universities according to the TUC (2019a), and if they refuse, you can go through their grievance procedures. Sending the worker or student back into such situations without it having been dealt with to ensure it does not happen again could also be seen as a breach of the employer's duties of care.

Responses to staff and to service users

In the BASW (2018a) survey, responses to abuse and harassment were often seen to be ineffective:

> *Regardless of the threat or way we are treated or spoken to we are expected to continue working with the clients. At times a zero-tolerance letter will be issued by managers, but this usually has no impact as is just words and the clients know they can get away with their conduct* (Family and Childcare Social Worker) (BASW 2018a: 9).

The report recommends that employers encourage staff to report to the police intimidating, threatening or violent incidents, that these should be taken to court by the Crown Prosecution Service, and that employers should support social workers throughout the legal process. Where a social worker has experienced intimidation, threats or violence, employers must facilitate the transfer of cases to other staff if this is the preference of the social worker.

Employers' duties

Staff subjected to abuse and harassment may not receive the support they need from their agencies, and attempts to work with the service users on their part in the aggression and conflict are not always a major feature in agency's responses (Littlechild et al. 2016).

As mentioned above, the Health and Safety at Work Act 1974 states that employers have a duty to ensure the health, safety and welfare of their employees, which includes preventing abuse, harassment and bullying. This is the case for any risk to an employee's health and safety at work, including psychological harm.

Building on this duty, perhaps the most relevant case to date for social work in this area, and indeed all employers/employees, is Walker v Northumberland County Council (Tes 1995). In that case, the High Court ordered the county council to pay damages to an ex-employee, John Walker, a team manager in child protection work, on the basis that as employers they had a duty not to cause him psychiatric damage by giving him too much work and/or insufficient back-up support. The council had dismissed the employee on grounds of ill health. Mr Walker had previously experienced stress-related work problems, and the court decided that the council had not performed its duty of care properly, and damages were paid to Mr Walker of £175,000 (Clement 1996). This judgment is important as it clarified an employer's duty of care towards their staff, not just in relation to stress as in this case, but on wider issues where conflicts and difficulties at work are not dealt with adequately to protect the well-being and health of members of staff.

Responding to abuse and harassment

In terms of the models set out in Chapters 1 and 11, concerning the hierarchy of engagement and of responses respectively with service users and carers, most agencies' policies will aim to deal with matters informally, and try to settle agreements in ways which do not make matters worse – hence the ideas and methods of mediation and restorative conflict resolution approaches set out in Chapter 11. Where this is not desirable or suitable because of the nature of the situation, or where such attempts have not proved effective, then it may be necessary to move into other less desirable ways of responding, as set out in the two tables of responses in Chapter 11.

Supportive reactions from managers and employing agencies are important, to provide clear messages to staff and to service users that acceptance of abuse and harassment is not 'part of the job', and to ensure that social workers feel they will be fully supported in their work on responding to these issues, and/or in actions taken to deal with the behaviour from the service user.

It is possible that the person presenting the problematic behaviours may not appreciate how upsetting you find them or the impact of their behaviour on others. There could sometimes be points when explaining how the behaviour is making you feel is enough to prevent it happening further. Only you will know – and maybe with support and trusted others to work this out – whether an approach of this kind is something you feel comfortable with.

If this kind of approach is not successful, or if you do not feel comfortable speaking to the person concerned, you should raise it with your manager – or someone more senior if for some reason this is not suitable or desirable, for example if they are the problem, or you have had experience before of them not dealing with such concerns. Set out what is happening and ask the employer to deal with it, keeping a record of your requests.

Reflective exercise: how would you respond to bullying and harassment personally, and in terms of gaining support from managers?

How would you respond:

a. if it was within a group care setting between service users?
b. if a colleague was being bullied?
c. if you were being bullied (see also Chapter 9)?

It will probably be left to the victim of such abuse to report it in the first instance. This is because most such abuse and harassment is carried out in a way that is not obvious to others. It is important to make a note of the behaviours you are finding offensive, when they took place and by whom, and to keep copies of offensive texts, tweets or Facebook posts. In addition, it is important to record efforts you have made to deal with the behaviour and get it to stop, and what the effects of these have been.

Where such abuse takes place in front of colleagues and managers, they should be the ones initially to discuss it afterwards with the person abused, to determine the effects of the abuse, and what they wish to do about it. They should support the victim to use the agency procedures to take this further if they wish. As we looked at in Chapter 5 on dealing with physical violence, victims may see the service user or carer as a victim themselves, of disadvantage, abuse in their own lives, etc. This can lead to the social worker excusing the behaviour, and not giving the message/ensuring their agency gives the message to the service user that such abuse will not be tolerated or condoned. Having no response at all to such behaviours can mean that it therefore becomes normalized, allowing that behaviour to be left unchallenged to be used again against other social workers and possibly other professionals. Agencies need to ensure that effective strategies are in place to support threatened workers and appropriately confront intimidatory and threatening behaviour. This means that colleagues and managers may need to encourage and support an appropriate and proportionate response to the perpetrator, as set out in Chapter 11.

Key points: TA ego states

In terms of your three ego states as set out in Chapter 2, you may want to check whether there is anything you can think of from your messages in your Critical Parent and Adapted Child, any transactions (including behaviours, attitudes, non-verbal cues) which are happening with a service user which may be engaging your Adapted Child, which mean you are not recognizing that the abuse/manipulation is happening. If it is happening, you may not feel strong or assertive enough to use your supervisors, managers and policies if you are not engaging your Adult to ensure that your work is not compromised by intimidatory and harassing behaviours. From your Adult, giving yourself a message that you have a right to be protected and have your agency protect you, you can try to ensure, as best you can, that you protect yourself, and that your employer is protecting you.

Court orders/prosecution

If the harassment is very serious, you can consider prosecution with the support of your employer, and/or an order to protect you under the Protection from Harassment Act 1997. This Act prohibits a person from pursuing '*a course of conduct*' which '*amounts to harassment of another*' and which '*he knows or ought to know amounts to harassment of the other*'. A person is taken to know that conduct is harassment if '*a reasonable person in possession of the same information would think the course of conduct amounted to harassment of the other*'. For more on this see Chapter 11.

Questions for agencies and social work staff to address in relation to abuse and harassment

Questions agency managers and staff can address in policies, procedure and practice are:

- How are limits and boundaries on different types of behaviour agreed, set and maintained?
- How clear are these to workers and service users/carers, and how are they best spelled out, reviewed, with whom and how, and maintained over time?
- What range of responses should be available, operated by whom, in what ways, from those who have the responsibility to ensure the worker's welfare and safety in response to such behaviours, to deal with any form of serious conflict a service user/carer is presenting against the worker?
- Who in the agency has the responsibility to ensure workers are supported in their professional competence and confidence as well as their well-being in order for them to be able to carry out their work effectively?

Reflective exercise: assertiveness in responding

From your consideration of your three ego states (discussed in Chapter 2), what can you identify that will aid you, or alternatively possibly limit you, in being appropriately assertive in responding to service users in relation to these issues?

From the same consideration of your three ego states, what might prevent or aid you in demanding appropriate support from within your agency in relation to these matters?

Conclusion

This chapter has addressed issues of how we can best recognize and respond to a number of areas in relation to abuse and harassment from service users and carers. We have noted that such behaviours relate to non-physical violence and threats, including abusive behaviour, bullying, sexual, racist, disablist and LGBTQ+ abuse, and harassment against social work staff.

The chapter has set out ideas about responses from yourself and your agency, including legally, in dealing with such matters, which can have such a major effect on social workers' practice, health and well-being. Issues of how you can further understand and then approach such situations have been set out for consideration in reflective practice, supervision and interactions with service users, and importantly in how you can best prepare yourself to make sure you assertively and appropriately ensure support for yourself in such situations.

Additional resources

In relation to support concerning abuse and harassment from service users and carers, see:

TUC (2019a) *Tackling Third-Party Abuse and Harassment: A Guide for Trade Union Reps.* London: TUC. https://www.tuc.org.uk/resource/tackling-third-party-abuse-and-harassment (accessed 14.11.19).

If you think you might have been treated unfairly at work and want further advice, you can contact the Equality Advisory & Support Service: http://www.equalityadvisoryservice.com/ (accessed 14.11.19).

The Equality Act 2010 gives certain groups of people protection from unfair discrimination in the workplace and in wider society; for more definitions of such behaviours, and guidance on dealing with it, see Chapter 9.

For wider sets of issues overall on these matters, see the website of the Equality and Human Rights Commission: https://www.equalityhumanrights.com/en/advice-and-guidance?who=individual (accessed 17.04.20).

7 Dealing with conflict between service users and carers: domestic violence and safeguarding of children and adults

In many situations in which social workers carry out assessments and interventions, there is a degree of conflict between those receiving their services.

This chapter will examine issues of domestic abuse and violence, and the associated areas of adult and child safeguarding. It builds on elements covered in Chapter 1 in relation to the dual role of social work and balancing out the rights of each of those involved in the situation, taking into account the service users themselves and others in their informal and formal networks, as set out in the Social Work England professional standards, and expectations from the two Chief Social Workers for England knowledge and skills statements for social workers (see the Key points box below). While social workers respect the needs and rights of all involved in a situation, it can be argued that the needs and rights of those who are most vulnerable as victims of abuse should take precedence over others who may be breaching their rights to safety and well-being.

Such abusive relationships include where psychological, physical, sexual, financial (mainly for adults) and emotional abuse, and issues of 'honour'-based violence and forced marriage are present. All of these can overlap and co-occur with issues of protection for vulnerable adults and children. These situations can then also be affected by issues of gender, ethnicity and culture (see section on intersectionality in Chapter 1).

This means, for example, that in situations of domestic violence or safeguarding, the social worker needs to approach the situation with an understanding of how the person being abused is experiencing this. In any of these situations the abuser(s) is/are likely to be using psychological, social and physical strategies to deepen and maintain that abuse, often using sophisticated and powerful strategies to ensure that the victim does not have access to support, by making them feel both powerless and worthless. If the victim does break the secrecy about the abuse, the abuser will often threaten to make matters worse for them by way of the abuser's subsequent actions, which we also need to try to understand from their motives and perspectives in order to do a full risk assessment.

The term 'victim' is used in this chapter to refer to someone who is experiencing violence and abuse within their intimate relationships. Often the term 'survivor' is used to denote the resilience and determination of people who have come through and are surviving such situations. This chapter relates to how social workers can help and empower victims to have a greater chance to see themselves as, and become, survivors. The challenge for social workers is in ensuring that vulnerable and disempowered people are given appropriate messages and support to work at their own pace to have the best chance for the situation to be resolved for them (Humphreys and Stanley 2006; Home Office 2015).

However, the dual role of social work discussed in the introductory chapter can mean that the social worker may have to take action to protect the victim even if the latter does not/cannot agree to this. Such types of situation can cause conflict between the needs and difficulties of those in the situation. For example, where a parent is experiencing domestic violence, the social worker will want to empower them to stop the abuse happening; however, where this may be a protracted process, their duties towards children who are living in an environment of domestic violence that may constitute potential or actual significant harm may have to take precedence (HM Government 2018). This would also be true where a vulnerable adult is being abused (Department of Health 2011). A conflict for social workers in this area means that, although in Chapter 1 it was set out how you should try to be as open and honest as possible in relationships with service users and carers, this could increase the risk for the victim or abused person in some cases. Your statutory/agency duties and Social Work England professional standards provide for you to protect a victim/abused person as a priority. These duties must override the duty to openly address the concerns about abuse with the service user and their partners or carers if this might put the person in need of safeguarding at risk in some way, so this has to be done in a way which protects the safety of the victim, as addressed in the next section.

Key points: balancing the rights of individuals against the rights of others

1. Key points from the two Chief Social Workers for England knowledge and skills statements for social workers on balancing up the rights of individuals against the rights of others are:

   a. *For Adult Services* (Department of Health 2015):

      ***Safeguarding**: Social workers must be able to recognise the risk indicators of different forms of abuse and neglect and their impact on individuals, their families or their support networks and should prioritise the protection of children and adults in vulnerable situations whenever necessary.*

   b. *For Child and Family practitioners* (Department for Education 2018b) sets out how social workers should:

      Act respectfully even when people are angry, hostile and resistant to change. Manage tensions between parents, carers and family members, in ways that show persistence, determination and professional confidence . . .

      Identify concerning adult behaviours that may indicate risk or increasing risk to children. Assess the likely impact on, and inter-relationship between, parenting and child development. Recognise and act upon escalating social needs and risks, helping to ensure that vulnerable adults are safeguarded and that a child is protected, and their best interests always prioritised . . .

Recognise and address behaviour that may indicate resistance to change, ambivalent or selective cooperation with services, and recognise when there is a need for immediate action, and what other steps can be taken to protect children.

2. Key points from Social Work England's professional standards:

   As a social worker, I will not abuse, neglect, discriminate, exploit or harm anyone, or condone this by others . . .

   [I will] *Recognise the risk indicators of different forms of abuse at home and neglect and their impact on people, their families and their support networks*

Power, control and secrecy

In order to put into practice the Social Work England standards and the knowledge and skills statements, it is important to be aware of issues of power, control and secrecy in abuse situations, where violence and coercive control frequently develop over time and become more pervasive and disempowering. At the start of the relationship a person may seem caring, and seemingly provide support and love. Gradually, over time, the perpetrator(s) can make the victim feel that they have to be entirely dependent on the abuser, and isolate the victim from friendship networks and family. This is intended to lead to a lack of self-confidence and feelings of powerlessness, with victims often made to feel as though the abuse is their own fault, and that they are unworthy of support. This makes it very difficult for someone to get to the point where they feel they have a right to stop the abuse, and/or are able to remove themselves from the relationship.

In its practical advice, based on its meta-analysis of evidence in the area of domestic violence, set out for those over 16 in relation to other family members but also applicable to children in most respects, NICE sets out best responses (see Key points box).

Key points: if the person is reluctant to disclose domestic violence and abuse

- *Advise that you are available to talk if and when they are ready.*
- *Provide information on help and support groups.*
- *Be aware of reasons why people may be reluctant to disclose domestic violence and abuse, including:*
  - *Fear of retribution from the perpetrator of the abuse.*
  - *Fear of causing a family breakdown or bringing dishonour to the family, or that their children may be removed from their care, or of an unsympathetic response, and/or of not being believed.*

- *Shame or embarrassment.*
- *Cultural stigma.*
- *Not believing that anything can be done to help them.*
- *Believing that the experience is 'too trivial' to mention.*

(NICE 2018a)

Domestic violence or safeguarding issues can happen in any socio-economic group, and in any ethnic group. It has no respect for employment status or other social or economic attributes (Lubker 2004; Thiara and Breslin 2006; NICE 2014; BASWO, Welsh Government 2018a). While there may be cultural differences in the contexts in which these processes take place (Thiara and Breslin 2006; Nixon and Humphreys 2010; Office for National Statistics 2018), the basic generic issue for social workers concerning people subject to such abuse relates to disempowerment of the victim (BASWO, Welsh Government 2018b). In addition, if someone is from a disadvantaged group, in terms of their financial capacity to move away from the abuser, this is even more difficult than for those from other more advantaged socio-economic groups (see the section in Chapter 1 on intersectionality).

Domestic violence and conflict within families: evidence-informed issues

NICE's definition of domestic violence and abuse (NICE 2014: 41) is '*any incident or pattern of incidents of controlling, coercive or threatening behaviour, violence or abuse between those aged 16 or over who are, or have been, intimate partners or are family members*'. This includes psychological, physical, sexual, financial and emotional abuse, honour-based violence and forced marriage.

The NICE guidance highlights how both women and men can be subject to this type of violence, in same-sex relationships and heterosexual relationships. Heterosexual women were generally found to be at risk of more severe violence and repeated physical violence; more injuries; more sexual violence; more coercive control; and to have greater fear of their partner. Women are also more likely than men to experience repeated partner abuse, abuse over a longer period of time, and more severe abuse (Smith et al. 2010). Women's reports of partner abuse indicate that it is part of a system of fear and coercive control (Hester and Westmarland 2005; Hester 2013). However, nearly 40 per cent of people who are bisexual, gay and lesbian in one study reported experiencing domestic violence (Donovan et al. 2006).

In relation to social workers recognizing signs of such abuse, NICE recommends an adapted version of the indicators produced by Black (2011) for use with different groups of people over 16, but which also apply to younger people living in situations of abuse and control. It also sets out knowledge about the best ways to respond, providing valuable knowledge for social workers on intervening in such situations where conflicts are arising.

Behavioural signs can include:

- symptoms of depression, anxiety, post-traumatic stress disorder, sleep disorders
- suicidal tendencies or self-harming
- alcohol or other substance use
- unexplained chronic pain
- traumatic injury, particularly if repeated and with vague or implausible explanations
- repeated health consultations with no clear diagnosis
- intrusive 'other person' in consultations, including partner/husband, parent, grandparent or an adult child (for elder abuse)

These intersectional crossover points become of particular importance when we take into account that the most frequently reported form of trauma for children is domestic violence between parents (Meltzer et al. 2009), and how there is a strong association between domestic violence and other forms of child abuse and maltreatment. Living in a household where there is such a regime of intimidation, control and violence was found to have long-term negative impacts on mental, emotional and psychological health, as well social and educational development (NICE 2014).

Coercive and controlling behaviour

The Serious Crime Act 2015 creates an offence of controlling or coercive behaviour in intimate or familial relationships (Home Office 2015). This '*does not relate to a single incident, it is a purposeful pattern of behaviour which takes place over time in order for one individual to exert power, control or coercion over another*' (Home Office 2015: 3). It is behaviour which takes place '*repeatedly or continuously*', and where the victim and alleged perpetrator are '*personally connected*'. There has to be a '*serious effect*' on the victim, causing them to fear that violence will be used against them on at least two occasions, or for it to have a substantial adverse effect on the victim's day-to-day activities. The alleged perpetrator must be shown to have known, or '*ought to have known*', that the behaviour would have a serious effect on the victim.

Key points: definitions of coercive and controlling behaviour

The Home Office's 2015 definition of domestic violence and abuse includes controlling or coercive behaviour.

Controlling behaviour is '*a range of acts designed to make a person subordinate and/or dependent by isolating them from sources of support, exploiting their resources and capacities for personal gain, depriving them of the means needed for independence, resistance and escape and regulating their everyday behaviour*'.

Coercive behaviour is '*a continuing act or a pattern of acts of assault, threats, humiliation and intimidation or other abuse that is used to harm, punish, or frighten their victim*'.

(Home Office 2015: 3)

Controlling or coercive behaviour should be dealt with as part of adult and/or child safeguarding procedures.

Reflective exercise: understanding the effects of coercive and controlling behaviour

Watch the following YouTube videos:

1. https://www.youtube.com/watch?v=XWvYVHiXqSg
   The Labour MP Rosie Duffield's 2019 account to the House of Commons of her own experience of domestic abuse/coercive control, described by the Speaker of the House of Commons as one of the most harrowing and moving contributions ever given in Parliament.
2. Experience of abuse towards a mother and her children: https://www.youtube.com/watch?v=NDWk-rKRTCs
   Consider how your views about issues of protection, ethnicity, class and socio-economic status may be affected by the issues raised in these videos.

'Honour'-based violence

There is no specific offence of 'honour-based violence' or 'honour-based crime'. It is an umbrella term used to encompass various offences covered by existing legislation, which can be described as a collection of practices used to control behaviour within families or other social groups to protect perceived religious or cultural beliefs and/or honour. Perpetrators can believe that a relative has broken their honour code, and shamed their family or community. It can be a form of domestic or sexual violence. The Crown Prosecution Service and the Association of Chief Police Officers have a joint definition of honour-based violence (HBV):

> *'Honour based violence' is a crime or incident which has or may have been committed to protect or defend the honour of the family and/or community.*
>
> (Crown Prosecution Service undated)

Adult and child safeguarding

Conflicts within families relating to abuse and safeguarding have become a major focus of both children's statutory services in England (HM Government 2018) and more recently in the safeguarding of vulnerable adults (Department of Health 2011). The Care Act 2014 makes adult safeguarding a statutory duty of public agencies, while the Children Act 1989 sets out criteria on which local authorities can intervene in families' parenting of their children: where there may be abuse of children through physical abuse, neglect, emotional abuse, sexual abuse, or most recently, living in an environment of domestic violence (Carr and Goosey 2017).

This has led to a decrease in emphasis on preventative work and universal services for disadvantaged families (Parton 2010). Social workers take the lead in the now predominant safeguarding work, putting them at the front line for potential conflict with parents of children or carers of vulnerable adults, within a social work role which is often investigative and 'blaming' from many parents/carers' points of view (Featherstone et al. 2014a, 2014b). This means projective understanding can be useful to understand the viewpoints, experiences and attributions of parents and children involved, based in reflection on your interactions with them from your considerations about how your relationship with them may be affected by your Parent and Child ego states, and your place(s) on the three points of the drama triangle. Consideration and use of these approaches can help us to be empathetic, assertive in making appropriate use of authority, and able to recognize potential for conflict and deal openly and effectively with it.

Child safeguarding

How might a child feel/experience the controlling dynamics of abuse? Vic Tuck (2013) examines how a child might be experiencing the conflicts involved in abuse situations and what professionals need to take into account in trying to protect the child's health, safety and well-being. Tuck sets out how professionals should ask themselves (as part of a longer list):

- *What it is like for this child, living in this family in these circumstances?*
- *Are these parents able to empathise on a consistent basis with the needs and feelings of the child?*
- *If highly resistant behaviour is being encountered, how exactly is this behaviour manifesting itself?*
- *What more does this tell us about the child's life in this household?*
- *What is the nature of the narrative we can construct about this child's lived experience drawn from our observations of him/her and his/her family; our direct communication with the child and his/her siblings; the parent's behaviour, and our subsequent hypothesising about the case and analysis of these circumstances?*

Tuck sees there is a need for practitioners to openly deal with power dynamics between themselves and families, and to give '*Demonstration of empathy and relationship skills*', but how at the same time they need to balance this with an '*eyes-wide-open, boundaried, authoritative approach aimed at containing anxiety and ensuring the child's needs stay in sharp focus*'. This then raises the issue of how we can best relate to parents in such situations, and attempt to carry out positive work with them, while keeping as our primary focus the child's safety, well-being and needs (see also Chapter 4 on these areas).

Adult safeguarding

The UK government's statutory guidance on the Care Act (Department of Health and Social Care 2016) states that '*Making safeguarding personal represents a fundamental shift in social work practice and underpins all healthcare delivery in relation to safeguarding, with a focus on the person not the process*' (s.14.207). In their *No Secrets* guidance on protecting vulnerable adults from abuse (2015), the Home Office and the Department of Health identified a list of different forms of abuse, including:

- physical abuse
- sexual abuse
- psychological abuse
- financial or material abuse
- neglect and acts of omission, including ignoring medical or physical care needs, failure to provide access to appropriate health, social care or educational services
- discriminatory abuse

For a fuller exposition of these issues, see the Additional resources section with the link to the *No Secrets* document at the end of this chapter.

Reflective exercise: experiences of adult abuse and safeguarding

Watch *Peter's story* in this YouTube video, where Peter shares his experiences of being abused: https://www.bing.com/videos/search?q=safeguarding+adults&view=detail&mid=D2B426C8358E21A58A66D2B426C8358E21A58A66&FORM=VIRE

Other valuable personal accounts of the effects of abuse on vulnerable adults can be found on YouTube videos, e.g.: https://www.youtube.com/watch?v=CA3ne394DzM&list=PLPYGYUQSmdUVpqT8ySISkwgYqDQygXb4U&index=2

1. Consider, by way of projective understanding, what the experiences, feelings, hopes and fears of the victims in these situations might be. Consider the same issues for the abuser, and how they might see the worker and try to relate to them, and why.
2. When you watch these videos, consider how what is shared might alert you to possible safeguarding issues. How might you proceed in engaging with the different people involved in the situation in order to make the victim feel safe and secure in relation to what you might be doing, and planning to do?
3. If you were the victim, what would you want from the social worker involved? What would you not want them to do?

Particular issues for elder abuse or maltreatment in adult safeguarding

The World Health Organization (2018) uses the following definition of elder abuse: '*A single or repeated act or lack of appropriate action, occurring within any relationship where there is an expectation of trust, which causes harm or distress to an older person.*' Action on Elder Abuse states that this definition has at its heart the '*expectation of trust*' that an older person may properly establish with another person, but where there is the risk that this may subsequently be abused.

The NHS (2018) has produced practical guidance for professionals on recognizing signs of abuse in older people – see the Additional resources section at the end of this chapter. This sets out the need to sensitively consider how you share your concerns with the person you think may be a victim. This includes keeping in mind that avoiding doing something about it, by trying too long to obtain agreement with the person to take the matter further, could delay protection and allow the abuse to continue.

The NHS guidance lists behavioural signs of abuse in an older person, including:

- becoming quiet and withdrawn
- being aggressive or angry for no obvious reason
- looking unkempt, dirty or thinner than usual
- sudden changes in their character, such as appearing helpless, depressed or tearful
- physical signs – such as bruises, wounds, fractures or other untreated injuries
- the same injuries happening more than once
- not wanting to be left by themselves, or alone with particular people
- being unusually light-hearted and insisting there is nothing wrong

Reflection point

Reflection points: risk assessments

As part of a risk assessment checklist, there needs to be recognition that some service users produce conflict in relationships by using threats/ physical violence/resistance and disguised compliance – for whatever reason – as a way of keeping other family members from telling others of the abuse. Some abusers may also use such strategies as a way of intimidating and threatening social workers so that they do not pursue assessment and plans to ensure the safety and well-being of the victim as much as they might.

Supporting victims of the different types of abuse and violence

Key points: important issues for victims in services

Important issues for victims are to:

- be taken seriously
- have people notice and act
- have people ask what they want to happen and work together with them to get it
- have people and services understand them – recognized and respected for what they can do and what they need help with
- be dealt with in a fair and equitable manner
- be kept informed of actions that have been taken and their outcomes
- have people work together to reduce risk to their safety and well-being
- have the information they need, in the way they need it
- be helped to plan ahead and manage the risks that are important to them
- be helped to understand the reasons when decisions are made that they disagree with
- have the people involved they want to be involved
- feel safe and in control
- have people around them notice and act early, if things start to go wrong

One key area in terms of adult/child safeguarding or domestic violence is to ensure victims can be seen on their own, and if necessary to use independent interpreting services that are confidential, and not performed by family members or others in their networks, as they may not relate accurately to the social worker what the victim is saying (NICE 2018a).

Should social workers always be honest? The example of conflicts in relation to domestic violence

The Social Work England standards state that social workers must be '*open, honest, reliable and fair*', and '*Make sure that relevant colleagues and agencies are informed about identified risks and the outcomes and implications of assessments and decisions [they] make*'. So in line with one other key feature set out in Chapter 1, we need to be open, empathetic and demonstrate concern for the person themselves in the situation as much as we can, while also being clear about our role in maybe having to pass on information to others in our agency, and to other agencies. This is done where we believe there is a significant and immediate risk to the person themselves, and others who are dependent on them. As discussed above, one of the difficult parts of this is that we know that, particularly for women who are subjected to domestic abuse and where they are also mothers, they fear that their children will be taken away from them as a result of the domestic abuse. They may not leave their abusing partner partly due to the difficulties of being able to provide for their children if they do leave; the partner may have made sure that they do not have any financial resources or family/friend resources in their networks to be able to depend on or go to (Humphreys and Stanley 2006). Parents can also be very worried where they may need to move to another geographic area, and what this might mean for their children and their education. Often such parents put themselves second if they believe that it is best for their children to stay where they are, even given all of the abuse. One of the issues of conflict for social workers is the latest addition to the Children Act 1989 in relation to significant harm, in which living in an environment of domestic violence can constitute potential for significant harm or actual significant harm for a child. This leaves social workers with the task of trying to best understand, and respond to, the dilemma of how to balance up the rights of the child, and the rights/concerns of parents.

We know that the way some abusers use their power and control over the victims means that those who are subject to the abuse can often find it very difficult to let others know about it. Therefore, if we were to be open and honest about our concerns when working with others in the family or others in their networks, this could make it more dangerous for the victims, and be used to silence them further, in order to ensure that the victim feels unable to share what is happening with others because of fear of repercussions from the abuser (Humphreys and Stanley 2006).

Reflective exercise: abused people's hopes and concerns about social workers

1. Using projective understanding, consider, if you were the victim of domestic abuse and/or controlling/coercive behaviour, what are the issues that you might be concerned about if a social worker became involved? Given our understandings about the nature of such abuse, and the dynamics in such situations, what might your fears, anxieties and hopes be in relating to the social worker in this way?
2. What would your thinking and motivations be in what you might tell the social worker, and what would the features/skills of the social worker be that might help you, or hinder you?
3. Considering these areas, how might you as the social worker best protect the interests of the victim?
4. Do the same exercise as if you were a vulnerable adult or an abused child within safeguarding procedures.

It should still be your aim to try to discuss with the victim what you are considering you must do and what actions you will take to protect their/others' interests, and discuss with them fully the support mechanisms for them in relation to their fears about what will happen if further enquiries and other possible actions take place.

These types of dilemmas can cause great distress for social workers in our professional roles. It can be valuable to examine your own Parent/Child ego state messages, within a consideration of how you might come across to others by the use of the Johari window/your possible positions(s) on the drama triangle. So, for example, if I have experienced such things in my own life, it may well be that this could affect how confident I feel to draw appropriate boundaries with both the abuse perpetrator and the victim. If I have been abused by a parent or maybe by a partner in the past, in my own learning based in my Critical Parent and Adapted Child, could this mean to say that I try to move things forward in a punitive way towards the perpetrator without fully taking into account the fear of repercussions for the victim? Equally, how might my own experiences affect my Adapted Child mode, if these may take me back to my disempowered and/or fearful places? Might this mean it is difficult for me to be authoritative and challenging of the types of behaviour the victim is experiencing? We can also consider from our drama triangle and Johari window perspectives how we may be seen by service users and carers, and ensure that our assumptions about people's beliefs and values – for example, in relation to 'honour-based violence' – and ethnic and cultural differences do not stop us from identifying and responding effectively and appropriately to domestic violence and abuse in safeguarding situations. See also the section on cultural relativism as opposed to cultural sensitivity in Chapter 4.

Key points: gaining the trust and confidence of victims

Key areas in order to gain trust are to ensure the victim experiences that they can come, in their own time and at their own pace, to be confident that the social worker is there for them; that the social worker understands the dynamics of the type of situation that the victim is in, so therefore will not make matters worse for them; and they will go at the pace of the person concerning any disclosures and actions, unless there is an urgent risk, as there might be in some domestic violence and safeguarding situations.

Conclusion

This chapter has examined areas of knowledge, policy and legislation in relation to how someone in an abusive intimate relationship may be experiencing that abuse, and how someone who is a victim of such behaviours might fear further repercussions/negative consequences as a result of engagement with social workers and other agencies. This requires us as social workers to understand our own approaches and agency functions in relation to such dynamics, and consider how best, from an understanding of the position of the victim, we can provide appropriate authoritative and sensitive support in trying to move forward to help the person be free from that abuse.

Additional resources

Vulnerable adults: The NHS has produced useful guidance for practitioners on different forms of abuse and neglect in relation to vulnerable adults, and responding to their needs. See https://www.nhs.uk/conditions/social-care-and-support-guide/help-from-social-services-and-charities/abuse-and-neglect-vulnerable-adults/ (accessed 17.04.20).

For ideas on how to consider some of the dilemmas involved in safeguarding vulnerable adults, see the Social Care Institute for Excellence's (SCIE) *Adult safeguarding practice questions* (2018), https://www.scie.org.uk/safeguarding/adults/practice/questions (accessed 17.04.20), within its wider advice on *The Care Act: safeguarding adults* (2016).

No Secrets, at https://www.gov.uk/government/publications/no-secrets-guidance-on-protecting-vulnerable-adults-in-care (accessed 17.04.20), is a valuable guide to the key principles for identifying and responding to abuse of vulnerable adults, although as official guidance it was repealed in 2015 by the Care Act 2014, which made mandatory requirements in relation to adult safeguarding.

The National Institute for Health and Care Excellence's guidance on domestic violence and abuse (NICE 2014) sets out some of the best ways to attempt to recognize the risk factors for such situations, including medical indicators, and how to respond to such issues. See https://www.nice.org.uk/guidance/ph50/resources/domestic-violence-and-abuse-multiagency-working-pdf-1996411687621 (accessed 17.04.20).

For key issues about requirements on professionals and agencies in relation to child safeguarding in England, risk factors and practice guidance, see the Department of Health's 2018 *Working Together Under the Children Act, 1989: A Guide to Arrangements for Inter-agency Co-operation for the Protection of Children from Abuse*, https://www.gov.uk/government/publications/working-together-to-safeguard-children--2 (accessed 17.04.20).

The Crown Prosecution Service website contains contact details for organizations that can provide advice and support on honour-based violence, honour-based crime and forced marriage in each of the four nations of the UK – see: https://www.cps.gov.uk/publication/honour-based-violence-and-forced-marriage (accessed 17.04.20). Useful advice on this for the general public and professionals is also available from the organization Refuge: https://www.refuge.org.uk/our-work/forms-of-violence-and-abuse/honour-based-violence/ (accessed 17.04.20).

8 Recognizing and working positively with conflict in social work qualifying courses

Dr Karen Mills and Rose Parkes

The potential for values conflicts between students on social work qualifying courses in relation to issues of religious belief and sexual orientation has been well-documented (Berkman and Zinberg 1997; Newman et al. 2002; Dessel et al. 2011; Chonody et al. 2013; Melville-Wiseman 2013). This chapter explores a conflict that arose during a teaching session focusing on social work with people from the lesbian, gay, bisexual, transgender, queer/questioning + (LGBTQ+) community. It examines the nature of that conflict, the attempts to mediate through the tension and the subsequent steps taken because of the learning experience. The chapter suggests actions to challenge prejudice and bias in the classroom. It proposes that a positive reframing of conflict can be achieved through the inculcation of a compassionate climate, and the development of emotional intelligence and reflexivity so that, while students may not share the same worldview, they can demonstrate respect and embed principles of anti-discrimination in their practice.

Areas of potential conflict for social work students with their tutors and practice educators are covered in Chapter 9.

The nature of the conflict

O'Hara (2011: 209) notes that '*conflict is a natural part of everyday living. It develops in both personal and professional contexts when there is a clash of interests related to needs, values, opinions, or activities.*' In this instance, conflict arose towards the end of a two-year postgraduate social work course. In a teaching session exploring collaborative work in the LGBTQ+ community, a Christian, African male made stereotypical derogatory comments about transgender men and it became apparent in subsequent discussion that the students in the classroom held opposing views. The appropriateness of someone who held anti-gay values and beliefs becoming a social worker was challenged by a number of white British female students. They could not reconcile this worldview with anti-discriminatory practice. Discussion centred around the ability/inability to separate out personal and professional values. It is important to note that, while this is an example drawn from a Christian, faith-based perspective and focuses on the issue of sexuality, our suggestions for resolution could relate to other areas of classroom conflict which are rooted in the opposition of views about personal and professional values.

Anti-discriminatory practice and strong religious beliefs do seem to act in opposition (Chonody et al. 2013). The literature reports that '*those with conservative religious views were most likely to express negative attitudes*' (Newman et al. 2002: 280) and that '*religiosity ha[s] been found to predict homophobia among social work students*' (Swank and Raiz 2010: 21), so it was, perhaps, unsurprising that this student held prejudicial views in relation to transgender people. Holley and Steiner (2005: 50) have defined a safe classroom as '*[a] space . . . in which students are able to openly express their individuality, even if it differs dramatically from the norms set by the instructor, the profession, or other students*'. While this open expression of prejudice towards difference was concerning, it nevertheless appeared that this was an opportune moment to discuss the value base[1] of social work and to debate the ethical nature of practice where tension between opposing beliefs had arisen.

Principles of human rights and social justice are fundamental in social work values. The BASW (2012, para. 40) Code of Ethics sets out that '*social workers should recognise their own prejudices*'. In this, the Code acknowledges that social workers are subject to conscious and unconscious bias, and a core part of social work training aims to openly discuss these biases. In addition, the Health and Care Professions Council[2] (HCPC 2016: 10), the social work regulator up until 2019, stated that social workers must treat everyone equally and not discriminate against anyone because of their personal views. The professional standards for social workers published by Social Work England (2019a: 3) state that social workers should '*Respect and promote the human rights, views, wishes and feelings of the people [they] work with*' and '*Recognise differences across diverse communities and challenge the impact of disadvantage and discrimination on people and their families and communities*'.

The need to address homophobia and heterosexism in the social work classroom has been a subject of research (Morton et al. 2013; Bernard et al. 2014; Dentato et al. 2016), but the same level of focus has not been afforded to what Hodge (2013: 249) terms '*religious discrimination*', where Christians in social work training face prejudice from secular students. In our example above, the tone of discussion was confrontational and stifled dialogue as students splintered into factions based on religious belief and sexuality. This was unfortunate because, as Holley and Steiner (2005: 51) note, '*[e]ncouraging students to speak honestly about their biases and unpopular views is a particular challenge in social work classrooms*'. This point chimes with one of the key themes of this book, which is about being as open and honest about differences as possible, in order to be able to respectfully deal with these in such situations. As positions polarized, students became less able to reflect on their own attitudes and responses to the situation. Attempts to challenge the initial discrimination by some of the students in the

1 We are mindful of referring to the 'value' base of social work, but acknowledge that social work encompasses a plurality of values, and therefore wish to encourage readers to think of this term in its broadest sense.

2 Readers should note that the Health and Care Professions Council ceased to be the regulatory body for social work on 2 December 2019 and was replaced by Social Work England under the Children and Social Work Act 2017.

classroom were just as oppressive and disempowering as the original derogatory comments, and this raised several issues for us as social work academics.

Issues for educators

The clash of values described in the classroom incident (above) raised several matters, including the male student's fitness to practise.[3] At the heart of the social work qualifying courses' 'Fitness to Practise' process is the knowledge, skills and character of the individual. These do not have to be directly related to performance but can include any act which may affect public confidence in the profession. Anti-gay messages expressed by Christian social workers raise the potential for the invocation of these procedures, particularly if they are publicly expressed (Grierson 2017). When applying these requirements to an educational context, the consideration of a student's capacity to learn and change should inform any assessment. We are concerned that any expression of prejudicial attitudes that is immediately referred for consideration under these procedures may close debate, limit the opportunity for learning and entrench attitudes. However, at the same time, we recognize that there is a duty to provide a safe learning environment and ensure that any marginalized groups are not further disempowered through their university experiences (Chinnell 2011). In law, the right to freely express both religious beliefs and sexuality are protected, and freedom of speech is seen as integral to higher education in order to advance student learning (Office for Students 2020). However, these rights are qualified under the Human Rights Act 1998, which means the state can lawfully interfere with them (if it is for a legitimate aim, necessary and proportionate). Since there is no hierarchy of human rights, as educators in this situation, where there was conflict between someone's faith and another's sexuality, we felt it important to work with each party to reach a compromise so that any limitation of their rights was proportionate and just. We believe that this negotiation and reconciliation is fundamental to the role of social work educators and practitioners.

The explicit teaching around discrimination also requires thought. Singh and Cowden (2013) examine the concept of 'cultural sensitivity' in social work practice and highlight how it is fraught with difficulty on both an ethical and philosophical level. Morton et al. (2013) explore this complexity through the example of sexuality. They argue that teaching about sexuality on university social work programmes focuses unhelpfully on establishing superficially 'correct' values in students and fails to address heteronormativity where the privileging of heterosexuality is paramount. Hylton's (2005) research found that such heteronormativity was pervasive in social work education to the extent that lesbian and bisexual

3 The Fitness to Practise process, as its name suggests, is where consideration is given to a student's suitability for the social work profession, both at the point of admission to their course and throughout its duration. Students are expected to ensure that during their course, including while on placement, they do not do anything that goes against Social Work England's professional standards, or the policies and procedures of their course or placement provider. Concerns may arise due to criminal convictions, warnings, disciplinary matters, or physical and mental ill health issues, but can also cover any behaviours which may bring the profession into disrepute.

students felt isolated and alienated from their learning experience. What is required, they suggest, is a reframing of sexuality and a stepping away from the notion of 'right' values to consider the way in which social interactions shape and reinforce dominant discourses in social work education. This approach mitigates against binary oppositions and creates space for open dialogue.

This lens can be used to examine other values conflicts, with the aim of avoiding a proscriptive interpretation of social work values, and thereby creating an arena for discussion and personal growth. Students are encouraged to respect service users' and carers' cultural, religious or ethnic differences and, at the same time, explore and interrogate their own and one another's value base and their concordance with good practice. In such an arena, the emphasis is on the journey towards a shared goal rather than the occupation of a moral high ground. If it is accepted that educators have a responsibility to protect the future service users and carers of any student they work with, then it is important to develop teaching strategies where conflict is worked through in a productive and empowering way. What follows is a presentation of some methods which we believe might help navigate the tensions caused by these potential conflicts.

Key points for educators

- Faith and sexuality can be a source of values conflict among social work students
- Social work regulators recognize the potential for personal/professional values conflicts
- Adherence to a notional 'correct' value set creates a climate of fear and recrimination in the classroom, driving prejudice underground

Teaching into the dilemma

Immediately after the conflict arose, we emailed students a research article (Melville-Wiseman 2013) and encouraged them to reflect on its key messages. The article examines the religious and sexuality-based 'schism' between social work students and suggests that it is important to find common ground and note that no one involved in social work education, training or practice is without prejudice. This acknowledgement goes some way to avoiding a 'them' and 'us' split in the classroom which is reflective of the 'othering' process that occurs when people discriminate against others (Powell and Menendian 2016). It was intended that the teaching team would follow this up with further classroom discussion; however, impetus was lost as the students involved did not attend the subsequent classes. This highlights the difficulties educators have in addressing conflict when it unexpectedly arises, as classroom time is limited. Furthermore, it is our view that reactive steps have a limited utility to heal hurts and resolve tensions once individuals are estranged and views are polarized. A proactive framework is required if educators and students are to collaborate in sharing ideas and addressing values conflicts in an atmosphere where all can learn from each other. As a result of this lack of success in immediately addressing the conflict that arose, after much reflection and discussion we turned our attention to future, preventative practices that we might adopt.

While our aim was to resolve the ethical dilemma thrown up by these contradictions and hold the students' anxieties in the learning process, the elapsed time, limited classroom contact and students' retreat from further engagement led us to consider longer term strategies to effectively manage future conflicts. Doing so required us to move away from a reactive position to one which pre-empted potential tensions, so we could raise these collectively with our students as likely areas for learning and teaching on the programme. We decided to examine our first contact with prospective students, during the selection process, to consider how we may revise our practice. During interview days, one of the exercises (a group discussion) was given over to the debate of an ethical dilemma concerning faith/sexuality conflicts. While we recognized that in an interview situation, where a place on the programme was at stake, applicants may be likely to disguise homophobic or anti-faith attitudes, we nevertheless felt that a discussion on such a topic required applicants to engage with this as a complex and multifaceted issue. At the same time, it laid down a marker from the social work university staff that such dilemmas, and the fractured terrain which they occupy, will be a feature of the course they wanted to sign up to. In addition, applicants were encouraged to engage with the fact that a human rights agenda, while ethically and legally essential to social work practice, may not be easy to adhere to where strongly held beliefs and emotions are conflicted.

Creating a safe teaching/learning space

Much is written about the creation of effective spaces for students to learn. Fundamental concepts include the idea that learning is an incremental process, rooted in the theoretical concepts of personality development (Piaget and Cook 1952) and involving the re-examination of existing beliefs in order to extend knowledge. This model can involve both individual reconstruction of information and a social element (Kalina and Powell 2009) where students and lecturers work together to develop new understandings (Vygotsky 1964). However, this kind of social construction is not possible where some students feel silenced or oppressed as a result of voicing their views (Redmond 2010). Gilbert (2017) develops the concept of the 'compassionate classroom' positing that, in order to accept challenge, students need to feel safe. It is only in a safe space that new understanding(s) can be integrated into the self to forge a new whole (Kolb 2014). '*When children and adults feel safe, they are more creative in their problem-solving*' (Gilbert 2005: 22). In our example, the classroom became an unsafe place; discussion was effectively silenced, and attitudes were driven underground where no further exploration was allowed. The group could not engage together in identifying ways to solve the conflict.

Having implemented recruitment practices that sought to address these tensions, we revised our induction programme to create a climate where disagreement and difference could be examined in a non-threatening and supported way.

The intensity of the early period of student life and its instrumentality in supporting students to 'flourish' has been noted by Vuckovic et al. (2019). Historically, induction (in common with other social work programmes across the country) has established ground rules for students' behaviours and the intended ethos for working together. It is a formula which students understand, and notions of 'respect' and 'listening' appear frequently on such lists. But these concepts are abstract and fragile and can rupture when faced with the reality of the classroom (Redmond 2010). They do not have enough specificity to help students overcome competitiveness and tensions in the learning process (Neff 2003; HCPC 2015; Gilbert et al. 2018).

Gilbert (2019) has defined '*compassion in the classroom*' as '*noticing, not normalising, the distress or disadvantaging of yourself or others, and taking action to reduce it*'. Page-Gould et al. (2008) found that when people develop friendships in groups, their anxiety reduces, helping to combat prejudice and lead to greater inclusivity. Feeling safe and supported by other group members enhances productivity (Duhigg 2016), and this increased functioning generates a psychologically healthier space for learning. Essentially, if we have a secure base from which to explore, we are more likely to listen to others and be receptive to their differing views. With this in mind, we decided to engage our newly arrived students in an exercise of 'speed-meeting' as one of their first induction activities. The task was prefaced with a discussion of associative bonding – that people bond most rapidly with others who they most resemble (De Waal and Luttrell 1986), and the rapidity with which this leads to the formation of cliques in the group (Gilbert 2016). Speed-meeting, and the active engagement with unknown members of the group, were explicitly introduced to overcome this tendency and help build flexibility and a collegiate atmosphere. The activity is well-suited to the early part of induction, being fun, fast-paced and low-risk.

The content of discussion is less important than the act of engagement, so every time a student faces a new partner, the instructions to 'make eye contact', 'smile', 'shake hands' and 'name oneself' is constant. These formal connections work on many levels: breaking down cliques, helping individuals to form new bonds (Gilbert 2016, 2017) and supporting less confident students to feel less anxious about speaking with others. At the end of the activity, the facilitator gives another short input and encourages the group to use the exercise throughout induction (and beyond) to build connections with others.

During induction week, the facilitator takes responsibility for challenging people who want to remain in newly formed friendship groups, encouraging them to move around, connect with others and accept differing views and perspectives as an important part of their learning. This is reinforced through input on Thompson's (2001) Personal, Cultural and Structural (PCS)[4] model and how language

4 The PCS model sets out that discrimination and prejudice occur at the personal, cultural and structural levels in society. These areas all overlap by virtue of the fact that we are individuals living in groups in society. It recognizes that, on a structural level, organizations can embed policies and procedures that are discriminatory, which are then enacted by organizations and the individuals working in them. Our ability to challenge this discrimination is influenced by our levels of personal agency, which diminish as we move from the personal to structural levels.

can reinforce prejudice or the stereotyping of marginalized groups. Other exercises emphasize the importance of celebrating diversity and developing empathy (Gerdes and Segal 2011). With this suite of exercises, we used induction as a platform for recognizing the importance of working collaboratively, the diverse perspectives in the room and the negative impact of taking the moral high ground in discussions.

We also model a willing and open attitude to be questioned so that tutors are seen as equal learners in relation to issues of diversity, learning from students and being able to reflect on that learning (Freire 1996; Melville-Wiseman 2013). There is an apparent contradiction here, as during the induction process the nature of the group is still fluid and the group's members look to the facilitator/instructor for information and energy/direction. Kisfalvi and Oliver (2015) use Winnicott's (1965) concepts of holding the group, combined with ideas of an alliance between student and tutor (Emerson 1996), to suggest that tutors can model professionalism and expertise and still be open to further personal development themselves. That openness creates a climate where mistakes are allowed, even inevitable, and trust that personal humiliation will not result from the exposure. The requirement to role model fallibility, learning from mistakes and being open to challenge are all key components, in our view, in making the social work classroom a safe space.

Social work is a rights-based profession (IFSW 2014) and, at the end of their training, universities confirm students' capacity to practise in an anti-discriminatory way. A safe space for discussion should not allow students to advance opinions without challenge or justification, where prejudice becomes reinforced and/or challenging ideas which are inimical to social work practice becomes impossible. Doing so may reduce tension in the classroom, but it also lessens critical analysis of ideas (Redmond 2010) and makes educators complicit in prejudice, stereotyping and the oppression of the people we work with. The creation of a safe space is purposeful, taking students to what Brigley Thompson (2018: 1) describes as '*precarious moments*' where topics which divide the class are discussed openly but do not contribute to trauma or the silencing of minority opinion. Instead, we offer a space which allows students to challenge and resolve internal contradictions between personal and professional values rather than either imposing beliefs on others (Fernando and Bennett 2019) or maintaining a silence which reinforces personal prejudice.

Key points: dealing with conflicts between students

- Dealing with issues retrospectively, once attitudes are entrenched, is not successful
- Tasks which enhance students' compassion can create an atmosphere where difficult topics can be aired
- Safe space should not exclude the possibility for challenging ideas which are inimical to social work practice

Practice learning – values in action

There are few social work settings where practitioners are insulated from conflicting values and beliefs (King et al. 2008; Leyerzapf et al. 2018). Social work is fraught with value-laden decisions. These can lead to conflict for practitioners who have not considered how their values may not align with the views of colleagues, other professionals, service users and carers – or, indeed, the wider public, where the discussion of entitlement to services in a climate of limited resources can lead to bigotry and prejudice, pitting the needs of some vulnerable groups against others.

The introduction of 30 skills days by The College of Social Work (TCSW) to social work education reinforced links between theory and practice, allowing students to practise skills and resolve conflicts in a low-risk environment (TCSW 2012).[5] Sessions offer an opportunity to capitalize on the classroom norms and mores of compassion which have been established in induction. However, some universities use these days as a 'gatekeeper', filtering out students who are not suitable for practice. Where this is the case, it may inhibit the open sharing of views. As a result, students' initial exposure to a challenge to their values may not arise until they are in their first placement, when such an engagement can be fraught with emotions, extremely stressful and, without the support of peers, an isolating experience.

In order to manage this effectively, the concept of compassion must be embedded in the training of on-site supervisors and practice educators. At best, practice educator training can develop a shared understanding of compassion and safe learning spaces; a requirement to be explicit in the discussion of ethical dilemmas and the encouragement to model good practice in this area (Stone 2016). Students then benefit from consistent approaches in the classroom and later on in practice placements. Once student and practice educator have been prepared for placement, the learning agreement meeting offers the chance to acknowledge, and address, these issues. Textbooks preparing students for placement emphasize the contractual aspects of the learning agreement (Mathews et al. 2013) but, while they are important in setting expectations, scope remains for the explicit discussion of values and how these affect practice. By confronting the interplay of personal and professional values in this forum, the tutor can continue to model an openness to values-centred discussion. At the heart of this approach is the

---

5 In 2012 TCSW reduced the number of formal placement days in UK social work programmes from 200 to 170. The 30 skills days were to be designated specifically for skills development. The new professional regulator, Social Work England, has altered this somewhat, designating *up to* 30 days for this purpose. Nor is Social Work England prescriptive about how these should be used, aside from saying that, along with placement days, '*The learning environment must provide education and training opportunities that enable students to develop their skills and knowledge across all areas of social work, gain required experience in practice settings and meet the professional standards in supportive, supervised and safe settings*' (Social Work England 2019b: 13). Universities have interpreted, designated and assessed skills days differently in their programmes. Skills learning can take place in a workplace or classroom setting and offer a mix of teaching and the practising of skills. As with placement days, skills days are mandatory, and students must demonstrate their participation in them and their learning from them.

requirement to foster self-awareness and the recognition of emotions, which are a fundamental part of reflective practice (Morrison 2007) through the development of emotional intelligence: the use of emotion to guide thinking and action (Neff 2003). Developing the ability to recognize emotions in oneself and others opens the possibility for dialogue and empathetic responses.

In the practice context, this might be theorized as 'reflexivity' (defined by Donati and Archer (2015: 62) as '*the regular exercise of the mental ability . . . to consider themselves in relation to their (social) contexts and vice versa*'). This reflexivity can be overlooked as practice educators and line managers use reflection as a tool for managing and improving performance, but we feel that emphasizing the importance of reflexivity at the learning agreement meeting establishes a mechanism for examining the way in which the relational and personal biases affect the dynamics of social work relationships in the practice context (Jude 2018; Watts 2019).

A student on placement is at the beginning of their learning journey (HCPC 2017: 3.3), and the incremental development of skills is intrinsic to this process (Tompsett et al. 2017). We argue that social work values should be seen in the same way: experimentation and getting things 'wrong' are a part of that process. When learning takes place in practice, however, the impact of that learning on service users must be factored in. The '*precarious moments*' noted above may still occur and be more vivid in practice than in the classroom. These should be deconstructed in supervision so that ideas can be explored and tested safely with ongoing support. Stone (2016) notes that practice educators are well placed to assist in this process. With the right support from social work academics, practice educators can help students engage in the interrogation of self, and others, which bridges the gap between a superficial competence and the genuine internalizing of social work values (Eraut 1998; Carthy and McGilloway 2015; Stone 2016).

Key points: placement and the social work curriculum

- Practice placements hold potential for advancing this discussion as they challenge values in action
- Learning to manage and navigate values conflicts should be a core part of the social work curriculum

Conclusion

As a result of prejudicial values and beliefs expressed in the class, we have reshaped our pedagogic approaches towards conflict, discomfort and anti-discriminatory practice. We revised induction activities, created safe learning spaces, fostered compassion and supported the work of practice colleagues.

In promoting active learning from values clashes and conflicts, we must allow students to be learners in relation to their value bases just as we accept that learning and development will occur in terms of knowledge and social work skills.

There is scope for teaching these issues directly, using problem-based approaches (Clouston et al. 2010; Boud and Feletti 2013) or models of active reflection with reflective logs or journals (Lyons 2010) to enhance learning (Brigley Thompson 2018). While the subsequent measures we have adopted to address values conflicts have not been evaluated thus far, we believe that a productive approach is to engage with the uncertainty and unpredictability of precarious moments. Sadly, our attempts to work through the classroom conflict that originally arose and led to our review of teaching practice were not resolved in the way that we had hoped. The incompatibility of the expressed religious beliefs in relation to LGBTQ+ people required a longer and more detailed response than our timetable allowed. However, this incident did act as a springboard for us to reflect on, and develop, our pedagogic approaches to working with conflict – both in the classroom and while students are on placement. It is our view that when such conflicts arise (which they inevitably will do), we need to treat them as openings where students can tussle with new and unsettling learning which, for us, lies at the heart of social work education.

Reflection point

Reflection points for work with students

- How can discussion of values fit within the crowded pre-qualifying curriculum?
- How should students' learning in relation to values be tested?
- How can we best protect service users and carers, as learning in relation to values develops?

Additional resources

For further consideration about ethical approaches to dealing with the matters addressed in this chapter, see the British Association of Social Workers *Code of Ethics for Social Work*: https://www.basw.co.uk/about-basw/code-ethics (accessed 17.04.20); and from a wider global perspective, the International Federation of Social Workers *Global Definition of Social Work*: https://www.ifsw.org/what-is-social-work/global-definition-of-social-work/ (accessed 17.04.20).

For further discussion about the issues in relation to students and their rights and responsibilities in relation to discussions in universities, see the Office for Students *Freedom of Speech*: https://www.officeforstudents.org.uk/advice-and-guidance/student-wellbeing-and-protection/freedom-of-speech/ (accessed 17.04.20).

For discussion about the expectations on those running social work qualifying courses and duties in relation to students, see Social Work England's *Qualifying Education and Training Standards 2020 Guidance*: https://www.socialworkengland.org.uk/standards/guidance-documents/qualifying-education-and-training-standards-guidance/ (accessed 17.04.20).

9 Recognizing and working positively with conflict in workplace settings

This chapter focuses on conflicts that can arise in workplaces in terms of bullying and harassment, and how you can deal with conflicts around these matters with managers and colleagues as a worker or student. In particular, it looks at various types of bullying and harassment – including racist, LGBQT+ – and how to manage these if they occur. Such bullying and harassment is normally considered in relation to work colleagues and managers, but in social work there can also be attempts at bullying, intimidation and harassment from service users. All workers have statutory rights to be treated fairly by their employers, including ensuring that you should not be harassed or victimized.

Bullying and harassment

Bullying behaviours are intended to cause humiliation, anger, disempowerment and distress for the victim. Bullying can cause psychological distress that affects personal, social lives as well as work experiences and behaviours (CIPD undated).

The Advisory, Conciliation and Arbitration Service (ACAS) provides free information and advice to employees and employers on workplace relations and employment law. It defines workplace bullying as: '*Offensive, intimidating, malicious or insulting behaviour, an abuse or misuse of power through means that undermine, humiliate, denigrate or injure the person being bullied.*'

The Health and Safety Executive sets out how workplace bullying is a pattern of behaviour rather than isolated instances, happening '*repeatedly and persistently over time*'.

Examples of bullying include:

- overbearing supervision
- constant criticism
- exclusion, for example from coffee breaks, relevant meetings and important emails
- being overworked and expected to work to unreasonable response times
- making threats or comments about job security
- personal insults (e.g. humiliation, personal criticism, ridiculing or demeaning comments)

While there is no legal definition of bullying, harassment is defined in the Equality Act 2010 as '*unwanted conduct related to a protected characteristic which has the purpose or effect of violating an individual's dignity*', creating an intimidating, hostile, degrading, humiliating or offensive environment for the victim. A one-off incident can amount to harassment. The relevant protected characteristics are age, disability, gender reassignment, race, religion or belief, sex and sexual orientation.

Examples of harassment include:

- unwelcome sexual advances or touching, standing too close, the display of offensive materials, asking for sexual favours
- intimidation – for example, threats of physical violence or psychological intimidation, misuse of power or position; it may also be where service users or carers are using tactics and strategies to intimidate – for example, threats, or repeated unfounded complaints (see also Chapter 6 on this)
- being frequently teased and humiliated about a disability that you have
- receiving homophobic/racist/disablist/biphobic comments

Such behaviours may come from managers or colleagues, or indeed service users/carers.

In a survey in 2018, the Northern Ireland branch of the British Association of Social Workers found that intimidation, threats and violence to social workers as reported in the survey were relatively common (BASW 2018a). While most reported that these behaviours were from service users, a number of respondents highlighted instances of harassment and mistreatment from managers, noting the extent to which this negatively affected them as a result of the power imbalances inherent in the situation.

Such bullying behaviours are often undertaken in circumstances where the victim has difficulty defending themselves – as is often the case in many situations of sexual, racist, biphobic, transphobic, homophobic and disablist behaviours.

Third-party bullying and harassment can occur where you engage with someone as part of your job who is not employed by your agency. Your employer has a duty to protect you from this. This includes service users or carers (see more on this in Chapter 6) and employees of other agencies (TUC 2019a).

Employers have a responsibility to investigate and respond to any such issue they become aware of, and to take all reasonable measures to protect employees from harassment: for example, if a service user or carer abuses a social worker because of their accent, ethnicity or nationality. All employers should have an equal opportunities policy in place, as well as a policy banning bullying and harassment of different forms.

Reflective exercise: experiences of bullying and harassment

If you or someone you know has ever experienced bullying and harassment at work, consider how you responded to it. Were there maybe any issues from Adapted Child/Adult ego states that affected your responses?

If you have not experienced it, how do you think you might react in relation to the different areas of bullying and harassment set out in this chapter?

How might you best respond in order to protect yourself and your well-being to a greater extent? Consider this from your thinking about your Critical Parent and Adapted Child ego states.

Effects of workplace bullying and harassment

The results of bullying that victims report are a range of physical symptoms, including a loss of appetite, difficulty getting to sleep or staying asleep, skin complaints, palpitations. They also include psychological symptoms such as anxiety, depression, burnout, low self-esteem, difficulty concentrating, moodiness and irritability. Employees can find their confidence undermined to such an extent that they are unable to continue in their work (CIPD undated).

In severe circumstances, bullied individuals may find that the ways they normally cope with the usual pressures of everyday working practices have become unsuccessful. It can be difficult, if not impossible, to find ways to effectively deal with the problem, and the person can regress to earlier learned ways of handling difficulties, which may include avoidance, withdrawal, crying, passivity, isolation and trying to please/appease the aggressor.

The effects for some victims can continue for months or years. The particular effects on a victim will depend on the nature of the incident(s), and the way the victim perceives it; thus, the same remark about someone's sexuality or certain sexual behaviours may be offensive to one person, while to another person who has experienced sexual abuse it may be very destabilizing and devastating.

Racist abuse, harassment and hate crimes

The Equality Act 2010 makes it unlawful to discriminate against employees or students/trainees because of race or ethnicity, including the different elements of colour, nationality, and ethnic or national origin. In severe forms it can constitute gross misconduct from a manager or colleague (ACAS undated a).

Race discrimination can take many different forms: direct discrimination, indirect discrimination, racial harassment or victimization. Race hate incidents are acts of violence or hostility against people because of their race and are illegal in criminal law. If these occur in the workplace, they are also unlawful race discrimination under the Equality Act 2010 (ACAS undated a, 2018).

Racist behaviour might include being called racist names, or experiencing 'jokes' and 'banter', receiving offensive tweets, text messages, social media entries and/or being subjected to racist screen savers.

Some key points from ACAS on how to handle the conflicts in such situations (ACAS undated b) are:

- Employers should intervene if they see or hear employees expressing or acting on racist views; incidents should be investigated and handled through appropriate disciplinary measures.

- Any employee who experiences racism – even if it is not directly aimed at them – should be able to raise their concerns with their employer and have the issue dealt with quickly and fairly.
- Employers must take all reasonable steps to protect employees from racial harassment – including from service users and carers.

Sex discrimination and harassment

Sexual harassment is unwanted conduct of a sexual nature with the purpose or effect of violating the dignity of a worker, or creating an intimidating, hostile, degrading, humiliating or offensive environment for them. It has been part of equalities law in the UK for a number of years. ACAS sets out how it can happen to men, women and people of any gender or sexual orientation. Equally, it can be carried out by anyone of the same sex, opposite sex or anyone of any gender identity. All workers are protected from sexual harassment in the workplace. Sexual harassment can include:

- written or verbal comments of a sexual nature, such as remarks about an employee's appearance, questions about their sex life or offensive jokes
- displaying pornographic or explicit images
- emails of a sexual nature
- unwanted physical contact/touching
- sexual assault

Some types of sexual harassment, such as sexual assault and other physical threats, are a criminal matter as well as an employment matter (ACAS undated c).

The Trades Union Congress research (TUC 2019b) shows that over half of women overall, and nearly two-thirds of those aged 18–24 years old, have experienced sexual harassment at work (TUC 2019b). Its 2019 findings about sexual harassment of LGBT (sic) people in the workplace – such as unwanted touching, sexual assault, and serious sexual assault or rape – found that seven out of ten LGBT people who responded to their survey reported being sexually harassed at work. A high proportion did not report this due to fear of being 'outed' at work and this having a negative impact on their relationships at work and/or their career TUC (2019c).

An employee may have a claim for direct discrimination if an employer fails to address homophobic, biphobic or transphobic comments seriously (Stonewall undated).

Students on placement

The same general principles apply if you are a student in relation to the issues discussed so far in this chapter. The difference is the power relationships/responsibilities, in that you may be concerned about how challenging such types of behaviour may affect your assessment on your programme. Your university and placement agency both have responsibilities to ensure that your rights are maintained in your practice learning area. Where possible, you should initially discuss the problems with your practice educator to resolve matters, while ensuring that your tutor knows what the issues are and how you are trying to handle them. If you are experiencing any of the behaviours set out in this chapter from any of the employees/volunteers in your placement agency, a professional from another agency, or indeed from service users or carers, your university and placement agency again both have responsibilities to ensure that your rights are maintained in your practice learning area. See Chapter 6 for more discussion on these areas.

If this does not work, then you need to involve more your tutor at your university, in order for them to try to resolve the situation. There will be procedures for dealing with such matters in your handbook and your practice learning handbook, which are important to follow to ensure your rights.

Where you have concerns about the responsibilities in the level of work you are being asked to do, about the supervision you are receiving and/or the support or assessment feedback from your practice educator, the same process needs to be followed.

Where, because of the nature of the circumstances, you feel unable to discuss this first with your practice educator, and there are good reasons why you are not able to approach them – for example, due to the nature of the power relationships and the issues that are occurring in the situation – you may need to go to your tutor first before approaching the practice educator to discuss and agree the way forward.

One other particular issue for students is where there are recommendations during the placement, or at the end of it, that the student is not passing. If this is based on issues recognized during the placement, there should be a clear agreement put into place with the practice educator, university tutor and yourself about what these issues are, and how you can be best supported to deal with them. This should be reviewed between you and them during the remainder of the placement, to come to a joint agreement on what will be in the final report. The final report will then go through a procedure of quality assurance at the university; procedures will be in place which are published in your programme and/or placement handbook, and if you disagree with how the processes have been carried out, or with the outcomes, this will cover how you might appeal to deal with these issues. If this is the case, you need to be in contact with the head of the social work programme, any representative from the student body on your programme committee for example, and/or with your university's student union in order to get representation for yourself in these processes.

Responses

Reflective exercise: personal responses to bullying or harassment

How would you respond to bullying or harassment personally, and in terms of gaining support to deal with them – and to do what – if:

a. You are being bullied/harassed?
b. A colleague is being bullied?

If you feel you are being bullied or harassed, you would normally be expected in the first instance to see whether the situation can be resolved informally, such as by discussing your concerns with your line manager or practice educator (unless they are the bully), a human resources person, trade union official or professional association. You may decide that you can address first the person bullying/harassing you – but very likely not. It can also be helpful to confide in colleagues about it, if you feel you can trust them.

If the matter cannot be resolved informally, you may need to escalate matters to a formal grievance, from which your university/placement agency/employer should investigate the complaint, within the relevant grievance policies. Usually, the grievance is lodged with the human resources department and/or your university/line manager, unless your line manager/practice educator is the bully, in which case you should lodge it with someone more senior. If the grievance is not upheld, you will normally have the right to appeal.

It is important to keep a diary of events, emails and other communications where you feel bullied or harassed, with details of the behaviour you found problematic, why, when it took place and by whom. Keep copies of any offensive texts, emails, tweets or Facebook posts. Make notes of the efforts you make to try to get the behaviour to stop, with whom, and what effect (or not) this has had. This evidence will be key if you are required to recall specific instances in any formal proceedings, but can also show that a number of isolated instances (which can maybe appear relatively minor on their own) are actually part of a wider campaign against you.

It is possible that the person demonstrating the behaviour may not appreciate how upsetting it is/sounds, or the impact on others. There can be situations when explaining how the behaviour is making you feel is enough to deal with it. This can be viewed within the hierarchy of engagement set out in Chapter 1, and in the model of a hierarchy of responses in Chapter 11. Only you will know whether an approach of this kind is something that you, in that set of circumstances and with that person, feel comfortable with, and if so, if it has worked when you have tried it – if not, it needs to be escalated within your university and/or agency as set out above and in the reflective exercise on responding to problems below. If the informal approach is not successful you should raise it with a manager or someone more senior, explaining what is happening and asking your employer to deal with it. Again, keep a record of this. Your employer should investigate your complaint promptly, including interviewing the alleged perpetrator and any witnesses, and ensure that you are not subjected to any more such behaviours from the perpetrator due to your having made a complaint.

Reflective exercise: responding to problems

Where the bullying and harassment is from a colleague, policies will normally expect you to deal with this directly with them, if you feel safe to do so. You need to think about who might support you through this, such as a trusted colleague, your manager/practice educator (except where it is the manager/practice educator doing the bullying/harassing, when you may well feel the need to go above them), your human resources department, trade union or professional association. Consider how you might approach this given your thinking about your Parent and Child ego states, and if there are ways in which you can be more likely to be assertive in an Adult way to produce the results you need.

Your employer may require the perpetrator to make a formal apology to you and to attend any relevant training. If bullying or harassment is demonstrated, a disciplinary hearing can lead to the perpetrator being given a disciplinary punishment, including, depending on the severity of the incident(s), a formal warning or dismissal. If you are a student on placement, these issues need to be agreed in how they are taken forward with the head of your social work programme.

Whistle-blowing

Greater attention has been paid to issues concerning openness and honesty when things go wrong in the care of service users and whistle-blowing by professionals in recent years, which leads to clear conflicts for them. Whistle-blowing is in place and required in order to protect the safety and interests of some of the most vulnerable groups in our society – service users and carers of social work services. The issue of whistle-blowing relates both to employees, and to students in practice learning placements. For students, issues concerning whistle-blowing will be explained in your programme and/or practice learning handbooks. This section will address your duties in terms of whistle-blowing, and why it is important.

Several important inquiries into the need for whistle-blowing have occurred in recent years, including the North Wales Inquiry Report, the Mid Staffordshire NHS Foundation Trust inquiry, and Winterbourne View.

The North Wales Inquiry Report

One of the key drivers for change in (all) professional regulatory codes, and the Public Interest Disclosure Act 1998 which is designed to protect social workers and staff in agencies where whistle-blowing may need to happen, goes back to the bravery and commitment of social worker Alison Taylor, whose actions led to the making public of abuse in a number of North Wales young people's residential units, and eventually legislation being enacted to try to protect whistle-blowers (Siddique 2012). In its commentary on the North Wales Inquiry Report in 2012, the *Independent* newspaper stated that the Report '*condemned the "cult of silence" that had kept it hidden for so long*' and that '*Had it not been for Ms Taylor, that silence might never have been broken.*' In its interview with Alison Taylor, reported in this article, she stated that '*A number of other social workers managed to live with it. One said to me that if I said something I'd be "committing professional suicide". But if I come across something morally wrong, I can't leave it. I thought sooner or later someone had to stand up and be counted*' (Clement 1996). See also the official government report on these problems in the UK government's Stationery Office (2000) *Lost in Care Report.*

Inquiries into failures at Mid Staffordshire NHS Foundation Trust

A key government inquiry in this area in the health sector – but with results relevant for all professionals in health and social work – led by Sir Robert Francis QC (the 'Francis Report', 2015 – see government response with key issues arising, at Gov.uk 2015), looked into where there were serious errors by managers and staff in a hospital. Patients had died as result of a culture of covering up mistakes and bad practice that put patients at risk, and where managers bullied staff not to report such errors.

Winterbourne View

Serious abuse of residents at Winterbourne View hospital, brought to light in 2011, led to a review of this hospital, and across England more widely, for such services for people with a learning disability and behaviour that challenges. A number of the patients at the privately run hospital, while such gross abuse was occurring, had a care coordinator who was a social worker.

Key points from these whistle-blowing reports

Key findings from the reports set out in this section include:

- Agencies need to ensure that concerns raised by staff are taken seriously and responded to, within a culture which encourages rather than discourages or actively covers up concerns about service user and carer safety and well-being
- If staff raised concerns in good faith, and eventually turned to whistle-blowing if those concerns were not taken seriously and responded to, in terms of addressing how the concerns of the member of staff raising the issues have been dealt with, there should be no victimization of those taking these actions (https://www.gov.uk/whistleblowing).

Public Interest Disclosure Act (PIDA) 1998

This Act sets out to protect staff from victimization if they raise concerns in 'good faith' about malpractice as defined by the law. It makes it illegal for employers to allow any of their workers to face negative consequences – such as threats of disciplinary action, damage to career prospects, and/or loss of work or pay – due to their making a protected disclosure. A worker is protected from suffering a 'detriment' or being dismissed if their disclosure is both a 'qualifying' and a 'protected' disclosure. A qualifying disclosure has three components:

- The worker must make a disclosure of information.
- The information must relate to one of the six types of 'relevant failure' (Public Interest Disclosure Act 1998).
- The worker must have a reasonable belief that disclosure is in the public interest.

A qualifying disclosure includes where someone's health and safety is in danger, a criminal offence has taken place, there has been failure to comply with a legal obligation, or there has been a deliberate attempt to cover up wrongdoing (Gov. uk undated a).

You need to ensure that you reveal your concerns to the right person, in the right way (making it a 'protected disclosure'). It should be made in good faith and you must reasonably believe that the information is true (Gov.uk undated b).

While the duties to protect and safeguard service users are clear, and to escalate concerns if they are ignored by managers, social workers encounter a number of problematic issues and conflicts that need to be taken into account to determine how to take these duties forward. A main one is where there is resistance from employing agencies and other stresses and pressures in relation to taking such action (Kline and Khan 2013).

The British Association of Social Workers (BASW) has produced detailed guidance on this (BASW 2014). In its Code of Ethics, BASW sets out expectations on '*Being prepared to whistleblow*': '*Social workers should be prepared to report bad practice using all available channels including complaints procedures and if necessary use public interest disclosure legislation and whistleblowing guidelines.*'

This may include, for example, situations where social workers observe poor practice in another organization or professional, health and safety risks, fraud, corruption, or deficiencies in the care of vulnerable people.

The first person to go to in order to raise initial concerns will be listed in the whistle-blowing policy in your employing agency, or in guidance from your university course. In only the most serious circumstances should you consider – after having taken advice from the student union, professional body and/or trade union – approaching regulators of services such as the Care Quality Commission (England), Care and Social Services Inspectorate Wales (CSSIW), Social Care and Social Work Improvement Scotland, or the Regulation and Quality Improvement Authority in Northern Ireland.

If you have such concerns, before formally raising a concern, you should write down the facts about what happened, when and where, recording any events in chronological order. Good records can include statements, photographs and documents which help provide corroboration to the truthfulness of the allegations. These may be used into the future at hearings, inquiries and so on.

BASW recommends that students, independent social workers and others should ensure they know their position in relation to whistle-blowing when they start their contract or placement and what support they can expect, for example from university tutors, practice educators, managers etc. Employers should have clear pathways on how and when to make approaches in their own agency, through to the regulators or quality assurance bodies, for example OFSTED or the Care Quality Commission.

Key points: whistle-blowing issues

Whistle-blowing is when someone 'blows the whistle' when they tell their employer, a regulator, customers, police or media about '*wrongdoing, risk or malpractice that they are aware of through their work*'; such actions are officially called '*making a disclosure in the public interest.*'

Social workers (in England) who make a 'protected disclosure' are protected from being treated badly or being dismissed under the Public Interest Disclosure Act 1998 if they:

- believe that malpractice in the workplace is happening, has happened in the past or will happen in the future
- are revealing information of the right type (a 'qualifying disclosure' – see main text)
- reveal it to the right person, and in the right way (making it a 'protected disclosure')
- they are making the disclosure in good faith and reasonably believe that the information is true.

Wider disclosures, e.g. to police, the media and/or MPs, are protected under certain circumstances.

Social workers should make themselves familiar with their organization's policy on whistle-blowing.

Conclusion

This chapter has covered a number of areas where there might be conflict for social workers and students in the workplace. These can include where they may be being bullied or harassed. It has also covered particular areas for students, where they may be experiencing conflict in relation to these areas, but also in relation to where they feel they are being treated unfairly in terms of support and/ or assessment.

Special consideration has been given to where social workers may need to consider whistle-blowing because of areas covered in legislation which the agency has failed to deal with.

Additional resources

Advisory, Conciliation and Arbitration Service (ACAS) provides free information and advice to employees and employers on workplace relations and employment law. It is also a valuable source of definitions and advice on different types of abuse and harassment: https://www.acas.org.uk/index.aspx?articleid=1461 (accessed 17.04.20).

The Chartered Institute of Personnel and Development (CIPD) provides valuable guides on how to recognize issues in this arena, including sexual harassment, and bullying and harassment, as well as providing lessons from case law in this area: https://www.cipd.co.uk/knowledge/fundamentals/emp-law/harassment (accessed 17.04.20).

Sexual harassment of LGBT people in the workplace is addressed in the TUC's 2019 work on this – see https://www.tuc.org.uk/research-analysis/reports/sexual-harassment-lgbt-people-workplace (accessed 17.04.20) – and in Stonewall's (undated) *Harassment in the workplace:*

understanding and spotting harassment in the workplace for LGBT people, and what the law says: https://www.stonewall.org.uk/harassment-workplace (accessed 17.04.20).

ACAS has produced a very useful guide setting out what race hate incidents are, and how to start dealing with them, in *Tackling race hate incidents in the workplace*, available at: https://archive.acas.org.uk/racehate (accessed 17.04.20).

Where to get support as an employee/student for bullying and harassment

There are a number of organizations which can provide advice on this for employees. For their members, this advice can also be found from trade unions and professional associations such as UNISON (https://www.unison.org.uk/) and BASW (https://www.basw.co.uk/).

The Department of Health and Social Care funds a free, confidential whistle-blowing helpline for NHS and care staff and employees who need advice about raising concerns, and for employers on best practice which is free, independent and confidential – 08000 724 725.

The Whistleblowing Helpline provides free advice and support for workers, trade unions and employers in adult social care and healthcare: https://speakup.direct/for-employees/ (accessed 17.04.20)

BASW has produced a very full guide on the issues involved in whistle-blowing and how to get support on this if it needs to be considered: https://www.basw.co.uk/resources/basw-whistleblowing-policy (accessed 17.04.20).

10 Recognizing and working positively with conflict with staff in other agencies

This chapter will examine what we know about potential for dealing with conflict in interprofessional and interagency working, in terms of understanding and application of policy, but also in terms of practice. This will include looking at the key issues of status between the professions, and information sharing. The chapter will in particular use examples of the issues raised for interprofessional working and trying to avoid conflict in these areas in relation to areas of mental health, learning disabilities, older people and people with physical disabilities.

Social Work England's professional standards state that as a social worker, I have to '*Draw on the knowledge and skills of workers from my own and other professions and work in collaboration, particularly in integrated teams, holding onto and promoting my social work identity.*'

One of the key policy directives from central government, and therefore for local government, in the areas of social care and health in the last 40 years relates to the emphasis on interprofessional and interagency working. During that time, ideas about interprofessional working, and motivations in policy to take this forward have been extensive, with many examples of this on the ground in local areas (Barr 2013). We see the commitment at policy level, such as in NHS England's *The Five Year Forward View for Mental Health* (Mental Health Taskforce 2016) and the UK government's mandatory *Working Together to Safeguard Children* (HM Government 2018). At a structural level, such commitment led to the instigation of the UK government's Department of Health and Social Care for England in 2018. However, the evidence about the benefits in relation to better working relationships, and therefore better services for service users and carers, is mixed (Frost 2013; McLaughlin 2013; Smith 2013).

Increasingly, interprofessional teams have been set up in areas of health, social work and social care. For example, youth offending teams within local authorities have been multidisciplinary for some 20 years, and can contain social workers, probation officers, police officers, mental health staff, and so on. The teams can be managed by any of the professionals involved. Frost (2013) discusses such issues of co-location of professionals and notes that this has started to take place in relation to, for example, children's centres and family support teams. More recently, assessment teams in local authorities that deal with referrals concerning children in need and possible safeguarding have become multi-agency safeguarding hubs (MASH) (Home Office 2014). Frost (2013), while noting that there is evidence to suggest that co-location can enhance communication, understanding of each other's roles, and learning together, also points out that while co-location can help, it does not guarantee effective joint working.

Part of proactive working with other professionals and agencies can include engaging with them in ways which allow discussion, for example around case studies, so that different perspectives, ideas and views can be discussed outside of personalized issues relating to professionals themselves or any particular service user and carer. Such depersonalization can be important to avoid conflict between individuals and agencies (Barr 2013).

The example of mental health

In the area of mental health policy and provision, this interprofessional emphasis has been the case particularly since the late 1990s. Since 2010 this has accelerated, with the idea that such interprofessional working would lead to an open exchange of ideas and skills and allow us to deal with service users' problems effectively and cost-effectively – the alternative being inefficiency, confusion and duplication (Bailey 2013). However, there are also a number of challenges in this area in relation to potential conflicts, for example:

- the absence of a shared philosophy between mental health workers on how to offer services, mainly around tensions between psychological, medical and social models about the causes and treatment of mental distress
- the development and influence of the survivor movement in mental health, which has encouraged the recovery model as a challenge to more traditional medical explanations
- a lack of common language/terms/understandings among the mental health workforce, with challenges about how the individual professions see their roles, and how this interacts with interprofessional working in order to benefit service users (Bailey 2013)

Bailey points out that there can be many types of processes in place to aid interdisciplinary input into provision of services, but there also needs to be the commitment to a caring and validating approach in the work, not just processes. If these are not developed and maintained, with the caring elements evident in the approaches to service users and carers from the professionals involved, this can lead to more distress, and lead to conflict with the service user and carers.

The example of learning disabilities

Culwick and Wallace (2013), in their work on interprofessional working for people with learning disabilities, argue that in order for there to be properly joined up services, they need to be planned and delivered from service user perspectives, with subsequent holistic services to meet their needs. This then becomes a key part of avoiding conflict in social work in such areas in terms of both policy planning and review, as well as shared decision-making directly with the service users and carers themselves. They argue that in order to provide services which meet the needs of service users and carers – and for our purposes in this book in situations that could possibly lead to conflict – there needs to be a focus among all the professionals involved on person-centred planning to ensure the rhetoric of individualization and empowerment does actually take place. They make the point that service users and carers can encounter different professionals each time they make contact with the team, and if there are inconsistent responses, approaches and lack of proactive work from among that team, this can lead to frustration and difficulties for both service user and carer. They make use of Sellman's (2010) idea about the willingness condition that is necessary in individuals carrying out interprofessional working, concerning the priority of meeting an individual service user's needs, described as '*the willingness to do whatever is required to contribute to effective team working. This includes a willingness to put the needs of the team on an equal, if not higher, footing than personal needs*' (Sellman 2010: 159).

These, along with the need for professionals and interprofessional teams to be committed to the rights, independence, choice and inclusion of service users and carers, can be seen as preconditions for planning to reduce the likelihood of conflict. Such conflict can be caused by a lack of personalization/caring approaches, and by technocratic and bureaucratic forms of professionalism and interprofessional working. The different languages used concerning delivery of care and the needs of people with learning disabilities, as also mentioned by Bailey (2013) in relation to work in mental health, is highlighted as a key feature to address in order to overcome conflict between professionals in learning disabilities services. Culwick and Wallace also emphasize the importance of different professionals avoiding role confusion, with, we could also consider, discussion about boundaries and where these can be usefully crossed/shared in a way which those in the teams feel they have discussed and contributed to in order to develop these approaches.

Culwick and Wallace make use of one of the key areas of work influencing approaches and work with people with learning disabilities over the last few decades: O'Brien's (1987) principles of working with people with a learning disability. These include community presence, community participation, encouraging valued social roles, promoting choice and supporting contribution, for example in assisting people to develop a greater range of competences. All of these can be seen as ways/approaches which avoid getting into an area of conflict that can arise from frustration and possible anger from people and carers who are using services.

Working with older people

In relation to work with older people, Lymbery (2010) considers how the policy statements surrounding personalization do not sufficiently take into account the complexities of managing a balance between empowering individuals' independence against issues of, for many older people, vulnerability and dependence, where the need for protection is becoming a dominant features of their lives.

Cornes (2013), in relation to work with older people considers – as do other writers, as we have noted above in relation to, for example, mental health (Bailey 2013) and people with learning disabilities (Culwick and Wallace 2013) – that the focus of professional and interprofessional working has to have as its basis an emphasis on providing an effective and personalized focused set of services, and a commitment to key principles of personalization, social inclusion, self-directed support and co-production, that is based on including carers' needs and concerns. So, in relation to issues of conflict, we can see that if we look at the needs and wishes of the older person themselves and their carers within the constraints of resources and sometimes bureaucratic agencies, these can create conflict all by themselves.

Bureaucracy within and between agencies can be frustrating and lead to conflict with service users and carers, and for the social worker themselves in trying to advocate for care packages to meet the needs of the service users/carers. In addition, however, where we look at the needs and wishes of carers, this may become a potential dilemma if the carer wishes for something different than the older person themselves – for example, in relation to the needs of the carer who is saying they cannot provide as much care any more, and needs the older person to go into residential care, when the older person does not want this. This is when social work skills of balancing up the rights and needs of all those involved, and working with other professionals and the older person and carer themselves, becomes key, in as far as possibly mediating between those conflicts of wishes and needs, in order to work out a solution, which may for example be in relation to supporting the carer more.

There is also a potential for conflict where service users and carers may feel that a plethora of different professionals being involved becomes confusing and worrying for them. In this situation Cornes considers that the role of the lead worker, who is the usual first point of contact and ongoing liaison professional with a service user and carer, is to be a reliable and familiar person who will deal with the life circumstances which occur around any presenting problems/ medical conditions there may be. Knowledge of local community resources, and professional services locally and wider nationally if necessary, can be important in providing the concern and constancy of response and proactive discussions about needs, and lack of this knowledge can become an important aspect of the development of conflict. In particular, proactive planning with contingencies to manage possible crises becomes a key feature in trying to avoid conflict.

Further areas of conflicts may occur where the older person wishes to have as much independence as possible, but the views of carers, and the assessment of professionals, means that this does not seem to be possible, in terms of legislation and policy. In balancing up rights and risks to the person themselves, and possibly their carers, this then leads to debates about whose rights and needs should take precedence. If for example the carer is suffering significant stress and is not able to continue, what does this mean in relation to their needs, and in relation to the needs of the older person? This then adds the need to address another area that could lead to conflict between social workers, other professionals, the older person themselves and potentially their carer, in that the carer could take control of the older person's budget and resources. This can have very positive effects, according to Cornes; but it could also cause difficulties, for example disagreements about the use and possibly abuse of that budget between the person themselves and their carer, as the carer may have total power in controlling what happens there. This could potentially lead to safeguarding issues, as explored in Chapter 7.

Working with people with physical disabilities

Donaldson and Sapey (2013) continue to develop the important theme of promoting autonomy and functional independence in the area of work with people with physical disabilities, the role of the professionals working with them being to facilitate this both individually and interprofessionally. They note the holistic elements which are key to social work interventions with all service user groups – and in this case, not only to do with someone's physical body, but also the personal and social implications of disability and how coordination of services between professionals and agencies is key to delivering what people need. Of particular note is the issue of the medical model, which has also been seen as part of areas of conflict in mental health work, in terms of ideas about diagnosis, and to what extent people are involved in their own recovery and methods of treatment. Donaldson and Sapey note how the medical model is built on the idea of health professionals knowing 'what is good for someone', whereas the social model is more inclusive, allowing discussion and dialogue about ways of supporting someone, as we have examined in the hierarchy of engagement model in Chapter 1.

As part of this, in one area of conflict in work with people with disabilities, which is also mirrored in mental health work, Donaldson (2009) sets out how workers who drew exclusively on theories from health psychology tended to explain non-compliance and therefore potential for conflict from service users in terms of individualistic explanations and pathological behaviour. In fact what is needed is further inquiry into the service user's perspective and the use of a critical social model of knowledge about disability – '*disabled people suggest that social phenomena such as the institutional environment, behaviour of the therapist and shared values can influence their compliance as well as cultural norms*' (Donaldson 2009). Donaldson and Sapey note that what is needed in order to understand the service user's perspective, and therefore provide treatment which is valid and valuable, is to use a biopsychosocial model of disablement that is a synthesis of social, personal and medical understandings of disablement. In this way, the schisms between different viewpoints can be acknowledged and worked with, to look at the different levels of need, how service users might be responding to the different ways professionals are approaching them, and dealing with them in the most positive and non-conflictual ways.

Key points: interprofessional working with different service user groups

There is potential for conflict through different professional languages, models and perspectives.

Interprofessional working should be aimed at creating an open exchange of ideas and skills in order to deal effectively with service users' problems and needs.

There is need for a clear focus on providing an effective and personalized, focused set of services, and commitment to key principles of personalization, social inclusion, self-directed support and co-production, that also includes carers' needs and concerns.

There is also a 'willingness condition' for individuals to carry out interprofessional working, which is about the priority of meeting an individual service user's needs – '*the willingness to do whatever is required to contribute to effective team working*'.

The role of social work: areas of possible conflict

While it is widely recognized that interprofessional and interagency working can provide real benefits for service users and carers, including improved efficiency, greater levels of responsiveness, and more creative and holistic services, there is also a real potential for conflict (Smith 2013). There are potentially concerns about role responsibility, and clarification and review of this – what is it your job to do, what is someone else's? How do you as a social worker set about clarifying this with your fellow professionals, and with the service users and/or carers involved?

In addition, language and conceptual barriers can provide difficulties, including how we actually view service users and carers – other professions may see them as patients, clients or customers – and therefore what this means in our different approaches and what it means for interprofessional working. So for example, in interprofessional working in safeguarding children or where a Mental Health Act assessment is taking place, there could be different views among the professionals involved – as well as between the professionals and the service users and carers – which can result in serious disagreements (Smith 2013). This then leads us to consider both our own view of our social work professional status, and how confident we are in using our professional knowledge, experience and values to present these assertively with other professions, and where necessary with managers in their and our own agencies to take forward our points and concerns.

Social work approaches, including empowerment, anti-oppressive practice, solution-focused (Dewane 2015) and strength-based approaches (Pattoni 2012), may not translate easily into the way other professions and agencies see what they are all there to do for service users and carers. Add to this the dual role which is unique to us as social workers, of care/control and balancing the rights between those involved, as discussed in Chapter 1, and it highlights that potential conflict is not just a question of the terms we use. At a deeper level it makes us examine what lies beneath those terms in relation to attitudes and attributions from professionals towards service users and carers, and therefore the understanding about these from the other professions. Possibly one of the clearest of such competing practice models is the apparent opposition between social and medical models in relation to people with physical disabilities or those who have particular mental health needs. Social Work England requires that a social worker '*respects and promotes human rights, views, wishes and feelings of people I work with, balancing rights and risks and enabling access to advice, advocacy, support and services*'. This means that a social worker has the duty to represent service users' and carers' needs, rights and interests not only within their own agency, potentially causing conflict here (see Chapter 9 concerning these issues on whistle-blowing, for example), but with other professionals and agencies as well.

Key points: interprofessional working with other professionals and agencies

In terms of day-to-day communications, the issues of language, terms used, who has precedence in determining the way forward, and how this then relates to the issues of status, present one of the most important areas for consideration in relation to the potential for, and how we deal with, conflicts between professionals and agencies.

Reflective exercise: projective understanding

Putting yourself in the place of a service user/carer, what hopes and concerns might you have about the different professionals and agencies involved in providing your service, and how they might (or might not) be working together?

In terms of these hopes and concerns, for you as the social worker/key professional involved, how might you try to engage with the service user and/or carer in the most positive way (given our understandings of the roles of advocacy, dual role of social work, and the need to balance up the rights of all of those involved in the situation we are assessing and intervening in)?

Again, from the perspective of the service user and/or carer, in what ways would you want the key professional involved to discuss with you how they are working with others for your benefit, and what would you like your involvement with this to be, and by what means?

Now imagine you are one of the professionals involved. How might this approach work well for you in providing those services in a coordinated way? What tensions or conflicts might you find with this, and how might you go about trying to deal with them?

McGrath (1991) puts forward the view that interprofessional working is not about 'fudging' professional boundaries, but about developing professionals who:

- are confident in their own expertise and particular skills
- are fully aware and confident in these areas of their colleagues in other care and health professions
- carry out their practice in non-hierarchical and collegiate ways

Allied to this, Smith (2013) states that each profession in this scenario must then search for their own distinctive rationale and identity. This can however be confounded by the roles and status of the different professions.

Hierarchies and roles

Reflective exercise: how do different professional groups see each other?

How do you think that different professional groups see each other? Where would you rank the status of social workers among those in the following list?

- medical doctors
- nurses
- police
- lawyers
- physiotherapists
- psychiatrists
- other professional groups that you work with

Consider how you think the attributions and rankings of each of these groups to each other affects discussions, whether your views are listened to, and why.

Professional status – in terms of how we view the status of different professionals such as doctors, nurses, lawyers, police, as well as service users and carers, and therefore what credence we give to those different views in interprofessional working – becomes important in relation to the use of social work models, methods and skills. There can also be areas of difficulty created by issues of status, pay, conditions and feelings of superiority from some professionals which can lead to difficulties. This can then impact on communications and decision-making in terms of whether it is an equal partnership between professionals/agencies. For example, in safeguarding children work, it is the key worker – the social worker – who has the main role and responsibility to ensure that all the professionals are participating fully in keeping up to date, in terms of passing on information and issues through them, and then finally whatever is in the child protection plan, and going to the local authority solicitor through the management structure to request – or demand? – action by taking the matter to a court for a statutory order to be made in relation to the child's legal status.

Engaging with interprofessional conflict: Exercise 1 – Conflict with a lawyer

Imagine that as a child safeguarding social worker you go to your local authority solicitor, who determines that it should not go to court, although you and your manager are clear that there is a good argument to put to the court that the child is at risk of significant harm or is experiencing significant harm.

How might you consider your role here? In terms of interprofessional working, do you accept what the lawyer says, or do you challenge it? What do you think the issues are in challenging a lawyer who does not think it should go to court? If you determine it should be challenged, on what grounds might you do this, and with whom?

Engaging with interprofessional conflict: Exercise 2 – Mental health assessments

Imagine you are involved in a mental health assessment as an Approved Mental Health Practitioner. You have interviewed the different people involved, including, most importantly, the person who is being assessed, in an appropriate manner. You believe that grounds for compulsory admission do not exist; the psychiatrist involved and the general practitioner become very angry due to the pressures they feel on them, and what they think should happen, and threaten to report you to your manager, and your professional association. How much do you as a social worker have confidence in your professional abilities and your knowledge in order to be appropriately assertive?

Engaging with interprofessional conflict: Exercise 3 – Assertiveness

In the two scenarios in Exercises 1 and 2, consider how it might leave you feeling in relation to your considerations of your Parent/Adult/Adapted Child ego states. How easy might you find it to be assertive in relation to a general practitioner, psychiatrist or a lawyer when you do not agree with them? Some people may feel in their Adapted Child that they have learned to defer to those with 'higher' professional status, while others might have their own views from Critical Parent about professionals who might take this stance against them, and become somewhat aggressive and/or demanding.

Information and data sharing

In the area of sharing of information across professionals and agencies, there have been long-standing and common problems in relation to the care and protection of service users and carers. This has particularly been the case in safeguarding children. In almost all serious case reviews where children have died while known to safeguarding children services, problems about sharing of information are present, within a wider set of concerns about sharing information and how this is collated and made use of. Some professionals still seem to think that there is a requirement to maintain confidentiality with service users and carers. It has been made clear by the government that this is not the case in areas of health, social work and social care in certain circumstances, as in the following seven golden rules.

The seven golden rules to sharing information

1. *. . . the General Data Protection Regulation (GDPR), Data Protection Act 2018 and human rights law are not barriers to justified information sharing, but provide a framework to ensure that personal information about living individuals is shared appropriately.*
2. *Be open and honest with the individual (and/or their family where appropriate) from the outset about why, what, how and with whom information will, or could be shared, and seek their agreement, unless it is unsafe or inappropriate to do so.*
3. *Seek advice from other practitioners, or your information governance lead, if you are in any doubt about sharing the information concerned, without disclosing the identity of the individual where possible.*
4. *Where possible, share information with consent, and where possible, respect the wishes of those who do not consent to having their information shared. Under the GDPR and Data Protection Act 2018 you may share information without consent if, in your judgement, there is a lawful basis to do so, such as where safety may be at risk . . .*
5. *Consider safety and well-being: base your information sharing decisions on considerations of the safety and well-being of the individual and others who may be affected by their actions.*
6. *Necessary, proportionate, relevant, adequate, accurate, timely and secure: ensure that the information you share is necessary for the purpose for which you are sharing it . . .*
7. *Keep a record of your decision and the reasons for it – whether it is to share information or not . . .*

(Department for Education 2018a)

In addition, Social Work England in its standards states that social workers must '*Treat information about people with sensitivity and handle confidential information in line with the law*', and '*Make sure that relevant colleagues and agencies are informed about identified risks and the outcomes and implications of assessments and decisions I make*'. They are also told to '*report allegations of harm and challenge and report exploitation and any dangerous, abusive or discriminatory behaviour or practice*'.

If you have any concerns about sharing information you should approach your agency's Caldicott Guardian, a role required by the UK government for just such purposes (NHS Nottingham University Hospitals Trust undated).

Key points: what do we share?

Key questions to ask yourself are:

- What do you share? With whom? When? And how?
- What can/should you ask of others concerning their information and data, for example about abuse, violence from service users/carers towards staff?

- In terms of planning services and sharing information, concerns can arise as to what others may do when we share information, and how this might affect what we choose to share or not. What are your feelings/thoughts about having control over information about service users/carers when you have to give information to other professionals and agencies? And how might this compromise relationships with service users and carers?

The problems and conflicts involved in interprofessional working are perhaps clearest in one major area of social work, relating to safeguarding children work.

Commenting on the lessons learned from Victoria Climbié's history of abuse and the inadequate responses of a range of agencies and professionals, the President of the Royal College of Paediatrics and Child Health stated: '*Prevention depends on collaboration . . . it is not just organisations, committees and boards that must work together. Children like Victoria die when individual professionals do not work together*' (Hall 2003: 293).

The UK government's *Working Together* document (HM Government 2018) is mandatory on health, social care, police and probation agencies. In terms of serious case reviews, where children who have been known to the public services as in need of protection have died, the serious case reviews frequently identify problems in interprofessional working and information sharing. The government document states that '*effective sharing of information between practitioners and local organisations and agencies is essential for early identification of need, assessment and service provision to keep children safe . . . Practitioners should be proactive in sharing information as early as possible. . .*'.

Key points: overcoming interprofessional conflicts at an individual level

Overcoming such conflict at an individual level can mean, in your Adult ego state, being able to state respectfully and clearly how you see the situation, and how you have taken into account the views of others.

It can be valuable to consider how you might come across in relation to such issues of potential conflict with other professionals and agencies, and from your thinking about your Parent/Adult/Child ego states. What do you think you might change, if anything, in relation to your ways of responding to, or maybe even creating, such conflicts? Consider from those ego states how you might be able to approach, discuss and suggest ways forward from assertive and respectful approaches from within your Adult.

Reflective exercise: how might you come across to others in interprofessional working?

In your interprofessional communications, might you be appearing overly aggressive, or alternatively too passive? Consider how your positions in relation to the drama triangle might inform your learning about yourself and your interactions with others in such interprofessional working.

How might the Johari window, and projective understanding of feelings, attributions and motivations of those other professionals, enable you to have greater understanding of these interactions and attributions?

Conclusion

In this chapter, we have examined how interprofessional working has become a key feature from government policy and multi-agency teams in local settings, and some of the particular issues that we can learn from for interagency working in relation to different service user groups. There has been discussion and suggestions about how you might view the other professionals and agencies that you work with, and how your approaches to those different professionals might affect your views, approaches and communications with them, as well as processes and outcomes for service users. Thinking about how you might make use of ideas from transactional analysis, the drama triangle and Johari window, it has been suggested, might be useful in developing your skills and strategies in this area.

Additional resources

The Centre for the Advancement of Interprofessional Education (CAIPE) is a charity which has the aim of developing interprofessional education, collaborative practice and related research, and offers publications and resources helpful to understanding more about interprofessional and interagency working: https://www.caipe.org/resources (accessed 17.04.20).

The Department of Health in 2013 published guidance about the benefits of, and intentions for, integrated care across health and social care agencies, with the aim of providing personalized care from different professions and agencies: https://assets.publishing.service.gov.uk/government/uploads/system/uploads/attachment_data/file/198748/DEFINITIVE_FINAL_VERSION_Integrated_Care_and_Support_-_Our_Shared_Commitment_2013-05-13.pdf (accessed 17.04.20).

11 Responding to workplace and service user-based conflicts

In this chapter, we look specifically at ways in which you can respond when conflict has gone beyond where you may be able to deal with it in your individual practice, and when you need to get others involved to support you. In this way, the chapter will look at generic methods for dealing with a variety of types of abusive/aggressive behaviours and conflictual situations that may occur in different settings – towards you from service users and carers, between service users and carers, from colleagues/managers/practice educators – which can be adapted and applied to a number of the different settings and service user groups in the chapters discussed in this book.

The generic conflict resolution approaches covered in the chapter are set out with the aim of applying these at the highest and most consensual levels in the hierarchy of engagement in Chapter 1, and using the hierarchy of responses model in relation to these areas as explained below. Where your individual approaches are not sufficiently addressing the issue, with no agreement possible about them and how to deal with them, then consideration needs to be given to the approaches within the lower rungs of the hierarchy of engagement and responses models. These then include informal and formal conflict resolution, such as mediation and restorative approaches. Again, though, if these cannot be used, or do not work, a move to the less consensual and mutually agreed responses needs to be considered, with managers supporting social workers in dealing with those conflicts.

Hierarchy of responses

Building on the hierarchy of engagement set out in Chapter 1, we can look at a model on how best to respond to conflictual behaviours. We noted in Chapter 1 how we need to aim to use openness and honesty as the main approach wherever possible, where this does not compromise the rights, safety, well-being and protection of service users/carers, or those of yourself.

Table 3 Hierarchy of responses to service users and carers (with the most desirable first, at the top)

Levels of conflicts	***Responses***	***Possible outcomes***
Level 1: *When potential conflicts/problems are recognized at an early stage between yourself and service users and carers*	Make clear your role, how you wish to engage with all those involved, and how, including issues of, e.g., care planning, resource allocation and/or safeguarding of those involved. Try to agree on what the issues are, the aims of working together, and how you might work together to achieve them.	The matter is understood by those involved, and how to resolve it is agreed on. If not, go to the next level below, Level 2.
Level 2: *When the strategies in Level 1 above are not successful and have escalated beyond this*	Discusses with your supervisor, manager or practice educator your concerns about the behaviours, linking this to any law and/or policies within the agency about such matters, and where relevant to the professional standards. This is in order to agree a way forward for the conflict to be resolved in the most constructive manner, if possible. This might include a meeting with your supervisor, manager or practice educator, and maybe also mediation or relational conflict resolution meetings.	If key issues and outcomes cannot be agreed on by those involved, look to Level 3 below if conflicts and tensions are great enough, where there may be a need to move to formal limit and boundary setting.
Level 3: *When the above two approaches have not been possible, or are not working*	Warnings, making clear to users of the service that such behaviours are not acceptable, in order to demonstrate to the perpetrator that the victim is being supported and protected. This could be by way of a formal, chaired meeting with the perpetrator, to examine the issues and set out limits and boundaries for all involved, and with possible repercussions if these are not kept to. This could also be by way of a letter or other communication to make these areas clear.	If these formal limit- and boundary-setting approaches fail and legal means become necessary, go to Level 4 below. Where possible in terms of the duties of the agency to the service users, consideration about withdrawal of services may be appropriate.
Level 4: *Where violence/threats/severe abuse are present that cannot be dealt with using the methods above*	Prosecution – check to see what your employer's policies state about whether prosecution should/could be pursued, and in what type of circumstances, and what support you would receive from the employer. Civil or criminal proceedings under the Protection from Harassment Act 1997 can include injunctions to keep the perpetrator away from you/your family. Again, check what your agency's policies might say about this and its support for you.	Ensure your safety and well-being by legal means if necessary.

Table 4 Hierarchy of responses to colleagues, managers and other professionals (with the most desirable first, at the top)

Levels of conflicts	***Responses***	***Possible outcomes***
Level 1: *When potential conflicts/problems are recognized at an early stage between yourself and staff/managers/practice educator in your agency or staff in other agencies*	If possible and you feel comfortable with this, discuss with the other person to see if it can be resolved. If not, go to Level 2 below. Make clear your concerns to your colleagues/manager/supervisor/practice educator, if you feel comfortable with this, and discuss at this level the ways that the concerns can be dealt with satisfactorily for all parties.	The matter is understood by those involved and how to resolve it is agreed on. If not, go to the next level below, Level 2.
Level 2: *When the strategies in Level 1 above are not successful and events have escalated beyond this*	Discuss with your supervisor/manager/practice educator your concerns about the behaviours, linking this to any law and/or policies within the agency about such matters. If possible, agree a way forward for the conflict to be resolved in the most constructive manner possible. If the problem is with your supervisor/manager/practice educator, you may need to escalate to Level 3 below, preferably after discussion with your trade union/professional association/human resources department/university staff on what the issues are, and how they might be resolved. This should include asking your supervisor/manager/practice educator to meet with the perpetrator to discuss the issue and ask them to stop. This might include mediation or relational conflict resolution meetings (see Chapter 9 on workplace conflicts, where these have been used extensively in work settings).	If key issues and outcomes cannot be agreed on by those involved, go to Level 3 below if conflicts and tensions are significant enough, where there may be a need to move to formal limit and boundary setting.

(*Continued*)

Table 4 *(Continued)*

Levels of conflicts	***Responses***	***Possible outcomes***
Level 3: *When the above two approaches have not been possible, or are not working*	If you are being supported well by your supervisor/manager/practice educator, discuss where or who you can go to in the agency next if the matters have not been resolved to your satisfaction, with their support.	If these formal limit- and boundary-setting approaches fail and legal means become necessary, look to Level 4 below.
Level 4: *The problems are still occurring despite support for you*	Consider consulting your trade union/professional association/human resources department/university staff. Consider if the matter might come under the Equality Act 2010, Protection from Harassment Act 1997, or any of your employer's policies on bullying, harassment etc. If so, discuss with a senior manager how they are going to protect you and in what ways (see Chapters 6 and 9).	Ensure your safety and well-being by agency policy means, or legal means, if necessary.

Reflective exercise: your strategies in responding to different types of conflict

From your considerations and understandings of what you considered in Chapter 2 in relation to your Parent and Child ego states, and your possible positions on the drama triangle and in the Johari window:

1. How do you, or might you, respond to different types of conflict with a service user or carer? How might you maintain open and honest communication about key areas and difficult issues, within their possible views of you in your social work role?
2. Think about what strategies you might use in:
   a. working with different conflicts between yourself and service users/carers
   b. working with conflicts between service users and carers, including taking into account projective understanding of the possible fears and/or controlling and abusive behaviours within the dynamics of abusive relationships involved
3. How might you most appropriately and assertively respond to conflicts with colleagues or managers, and in exchanges with staff in other agencies?

In previous chapters, we have concentrated on how you can best approach dealing with conflict in your personal practice, and when needed to call on managers within your agency to support you. The following sections set out methods for dealing with conflict where it has escalated to Level 2 or beyond in the models in Tables 3 and 4 above, and where you need to make use of your agency support and procedures to deal with the matter.

Mediation

Mediation can be useful where there are disputes between people in workplace settings, and in some service user/carer disputes. This process attempts to resolve matters and prevent them from becoming more serious (ACAS undated b; Caller 2013).

Mediation should be voluntary. It usually involves a facilitator, who is as far as possible independent and impartial, helping two or more individuals who have a dispute to reach a resolution on ways forward that are acceptable to each of them. The facilitator does not make judgements or determine outcomes; they ask questions that help participants to understand the issues and to clarify the options for resolving their differences or dispute.

The overriding aim of mediation is to restore and maintain the workplace relationship or working relationships with service users/carers wherever possible. The focus is not on determining who was right or wrong; it is a form of problem-solving/solution-focused approach. It can be used at any stage in a dispute, but is generally most effective before individuals' positions become entrenched (ACAS undated b).

In a number of situations and areas discussed in the different chapters of this book, mediation could be looked at as a first step in trying to resolve conflicts where it is suitable and acceptable to all, following proper preparation for the process with each of the individuals involved, and an understanding of possible outcomes. As with the restorative approaches set out below, there needs to be an assessment to ensure such an approach will not exacerbate the situation, with the fully informed consent of all to take part, and a risk assessment, to avoid making matters worse by making the victim be/feel more victimized (Littlechild 2009, 2010).

To look at resources to help set up a mediation meeting and facilitate it effectively, see the Additional resources section at the end of this chapter.

Restorative conflict resolution

Conflict resolution and restorative approaches can be important in dealing with conflict and hurt if handled sensitively. For an aggrieved person who believes they have been the victim of someone else's behaviour, including potentially abuse and harassment, restorative conflict resolution sets out to meet the needs of the victim in a safe, contained environment. The aim is to produce a resolution in which the victim feels that reparation is being made, and that the perpetrator understands the effects of their actions, in order to help them realize the hurt and harm caused. Whereas mediation tends to be more focused on disputes between people, restorative approaches tend to be used in situations where someone feels aggrieved and hurt by attitudes or behaviours of others, and perhaps where a complaint has been made against another. This latter scenario may or may not involve criminal behaviour, and may mean offering an apology for the behaviour.

Such approaches have a potentially important part to play both in resolving conflicts more positively, and in helping service users/colleagues to learn better ways to relate to others in current and future situations, thereby increasing the chances of satisfying and stable relationships, to the benefit of all concerned.

Key points: positive elements of mediation and restorative approaches

In restorative approaches, the aim is not to look to apportion blame, but to find means to move on from the dispute/grievance in a positive way, beyond the 'blame game'.

This can be done with the social worker and service users/carers/other staff in the agency, before it reaches a serious and entrenched phase, and can also be used, for example, in team meetings, where there are conflicts starting to arise.

Key issues to consider when employing such approaches are confidentiality; monitoring the experiences of the effects on both participants before, during and after such meetings; and ensuring any issues in relation to possible violence and bullying are fully addressed.

In a study of the effects of the introduction of such approaches into young people's residential units in one local authority, young people and staff found it helped young people to realize the effects of their actions, and develop in ways which helped them to appreciate the experiences of others, including:

- greater empathy towards others
- increased mutual respect
- improved skills for managing conflict
- improved anger-management skills
- a sense of responsibility
- more opportunities for residents to voice their concerns and feelings
- a feeling that they were part of the process
- an understanding that actions have consequences (Littlechild 2003)

Social workers have the potential to make such conflict resolution approaches key features in their methods, at personal, community and agency levels. By building on a mix of restorative justice and mediation techniques, relational conflict resolution can be a valuable approach in many social work and social care situations where conflict and disputes are taking place. For more on setting up and running such meetings, see the Additional resources section at the end of the chapter, with links to videos to help set up a mediation/relational conflict resolution meeting, and facilitate them effectively.

Beyond mediation and relational conflict resolution approaches

Critical incident analyses (CIAs)

This section looks at critical incident analyses in work with service users and carers, and the use of legislation and policy in relation to Level 4 in the model of responses set out in Tables 3 and 4 earlier in this chapter.

In terms of recognizing what may be important to learn from what happened in a situation, a critical incident analysis, involving a 360-degree examination of what happened from a variety of perspectives, can be valuable. It involves analysing and taking forward risk assessments and risk management approaches from such analysis.

It is a method whereby managers and the affected workers take time to systematically analyse the causes of the incident(s), and what now needs to happen to deal with and hopefully even help resolve the issues for the victim, and the staff group, or the service user/carer. This needs to placed on the agency's information system for others to see, and ideally should be in a form which allows the service user to have access to it/contribute to it. Indeed, given the evidence of how such behaviours need if possible to be addressed for the benefit of all, such recording should be seen as part of care plans and ongoing work openly shared with the service user, where appropriate.

Items to include in a critical incident analysis include:

- What were the triggers which led to the conflict – for example, physical space/ territory issues; risk assessment issues; the way the service user was approached/experienced the intervention, and so on? This needs to be looked at from each person's perspective (by involving the service user where possible, and if relevant and appropriate the carers, in the CIA) using the Johari window, projective understanding of the service user's experience of the situation, and their attributions towards you. Valuable for you personally but not to be recorded/shared with all here can be your reflections about where you might be on the three points of the drama triangle, and in your transactional analysis Parent, Adult and Child ego states.
- What had the role of the worker been in the incident? What support could they have had/should they have accessed to reduce the risk?
- What do we know of the service user's previous behaviours, which need to be taken into account in understanding why they did what they did?
- What attributions did they have/might they have had of the worker/agency role that may have exacerbated the situation?
- If it was a set of behaviours over time which gradually led to the problem, what were the behaviours which in retrospect could have alerted the worker agency to the risk, and allowed action to be taken to minimize its likelihood?
- What needs to be recorded, how, and who do you need to inform of the incident and the risk assessment arising from the critical incident analysis within your own agency, and other agencies?
- Does the recording give effective, fair, inclusive and just ways of ensuring the trigger factors for that service user can be taken into account for other workers?
- Were the reactions to the perpetrator sufficient to help prevent a recurrence from them?
- Were the needs of the victim/others affected adequately dealt with?
- Were the needs/difficulties of the aggressor adequately dealt with?
- How will you share the assessment with the service user/carer in order to address the issues in your work with them without creating greater risk to the worker(s) involved?

Reflective exercise: risk assessment and risk management

In relation to the different types of conflict examined in this book, agencies have a responsibility to:

- have clear procedures setting out risk assessment procedures
- ensure that workers are fully involved in this risk assessment process, to know what to do when there is thought to be a risk, if an encounter is escalating into a possible violent incident, and after an incident

- provide support in dealing with concerns about threats, abuse and violence, providing appropriate and timely support before an incident if it is considered to be risky, or actually during the incident
- consider what action to take with the perpetrator.

Think about how you might feel in a situation where you might have needed support in these ways – do you know what the policies and procedures are in your employing agency? If, in considering these areas, you have any uncertainties about how well those in your agency might support you, who might you talk to about this? And what would you want to say to them to try improve these matters?

Responses to the service user

Consider if the service user needs to be worked with/warned about the behaviour and actions that would be taken if it happened again. This may be by way of a formal meeting with the manager to alert users of the service that such behaviour cannot be tolerated, and to show the victim that they are protected from possible further victimization. Try to ensure that the matter is addressed and dealt with by managers. How this is done is important, ensuring that while making clear they are accepted as a person, and are valued as a human being, it is made clear to service users/carers that the behaviour is not acceptable, and how this will be dealt with between those involved, with the agency's support. Consider using the relational conflict resolution process set out earlier in this chapter.

Do consider with your supervisor/practice educator/manager if you should continue to work with the service user, and if so on what basis and with what agency reactions to ensure limits and boundaries are set with the service user. If this is seen to be too risky, but you still agree to carry on, jointly produce where possible with your manager (and maybe even the service user) a risk assessment and risk management plan to ensure your and others' safety. You may wish to consider suggesting co-working, at least for a short period. In practical terms, co-working can be seen to be important in dealing with situations where there is conflict with service users and carers, as it can take the focus away from you yourself as the problem/target. It can also be important in ensuring that difficult family dynamics and/or the situation do not overwhelm a single worker's assessment/intervention. It is potentially valuable also in modelling strategies and approaches for newer workers from experienced workers.

Key points: post-violence or abuse support

Is there post-violence/abuse support and counselling in your agency for you?
How comfortable do you feel in calling on this if it was needed?
What might you do to get to a point where you would trust these areas from your employer to a greater extent, and with whom?

Legislation and policy

Duties of employers

The Health and Safety at Work Act (HASAWA) 1974 places a legal duty on employers to, as far as is practicable, take responsibility to ensure the health, welfare and safety of their employees while at work, which includes preventing abuse, harassment and bullying. This is the case for any risk to an employee's health and safety at work (see the important case law re John Walker in Chapter 6 on this). The other side of this coin is that individual workers also have responsibilities for themselves in this regard under the Act.

There is an obligation on employers to make improvements '*as far as is reasonably practical*' in order to eliminate or control sufficiently any identified risk within reasonable financial limits. So, you should expect personally for your manager to ensure that there are both proper risk assessments and risk management plans for your safety and well-being.

Duties of employees

If there is risk in these ways, it is your duty to ensure you inform your employer of this. When doing so, ensure you have an audit trail of communications – so make sure your email is responded to, as you need to show that the manager/employer has been made aware of the risk, and how they responded (or did not) to it. This can be important later if psychological or physical hurt does take place.

Legal responses: court orders/prosecution

If the harassment is very serious, you can consider prosecution with the support of your employer, and/or an order to protect you under the Protection from Harassment Act 1997. This Act prohibits a person from pursuing '*a course of conduct*' which '*amounts to harassment of another*' and which '*he knows or ought to know amounts to harassment of the other*'. A person is taken to know that conduct is harassment if '*a reasonable person in possession of the same information would think the course of conduct amounted to harassment of the other*'. For individual workers, the Protection from Harassment Act 1997 is important to be aware of and enact in your personal practice, and indeed it can be used by social workers to aid service users who are being harassed and intimidated as defined in the Act (see Chapter 6 on this).

The Protection of Freedoms Act 2012 inserted a new element into the Protection from Harassment Act 1997. This is the offence of stalking, which includes monitoring a person online, contacting a person, loitering in a public or private place, and interfering with property or spying on a person, which may create fear of violence. You may apply through civil proceedings for damages or an injunction in respect of actual or apprehended harassment, or the police can take the order. If these are breached, warrants for arrest can be issued.

Prosecution

Support for the social worker needs to include not only professional effects, but also those in their private lives – relationships with close friends, partners and immediate family in particular may also be affected and put under stress by what has happened to the social worker (Community Care 2011). If there is a criminal offence in relation to, for example, harassment, violence, aggression or abuse under any of the legislation discussed in this book, it is important to discuss with your managers, and more widely within your agency if necessary, and possibly with trade unions and/or your professional association if you belong to one, about taking these matters forward, not least to possibly ensure better protection for yourself in future.

Conclusion

This chapter has looked at how you might view hierarchies of responses to the different ways in which you might engage where there are situations of conflict as set out in Chapter 1.

It has looked at a number of approaches such as mediation and relational conflict resolution that can be used in a variety of situations where there is a conflict between yourself as a social worker, service users and carers, professionals and other agencies, and colleagues and managers in your own agency.

Within a recognition that conflict can be at the heart of many social work roles to varying extents, in relation to the dual role of care and control and the balancing of the rights and needs of different people involved where we are intervening, this chapter has suggested in addition ways of how we as individuals might best approach such situations. Equally, if not more important possibly, it also sets out what we should expect and can ask for from employing agencies when set limits and boundaries are indicated or required in order to protect not only ourselves, but our service users and carers as well.

Additional resources

For more on mediation approaches, see ACAS (2013) *Mediation: An Approach to Resolving Workplace Issues*. London: ACAS: https://www.acas.org.uk/media/949/Mediation-An-approach-to-resolving-workplace-issues/pdf/Mediation-an-approach-to-resolving-workplace-issues.pdf (accessed 17.04.20).

For discussion about the use of mediation in social work, see the Social Care Institute for Excellence's guide on *Safeguarding adults: mediation and family group conferences* (2012): https://www.scie.org.uk/publications/mediation/ (accessed 17.04.20).

For planning and running restorative conflict resolution meetings, see examples on YouTube, such as: *A restorative justice meeting*: https://www.youtube.com/watch?v=dcTHYKX2LfI *A short introduction to restorative approaches*: https://www.youtube.com/watch?v=gJJxbn1VjYo *Restorative approaches to workplace issues*: https://www.youtube.com/watch?v=EXX-c_9cLwY (accessed 17.04.20).

The ways in which the Protection from Harassment Act 1997 can be used to protect yourself, and indeed service users if they are experiencing harassment, can be found at: https://www.legislation.gov.uk/ukpga/1997/40/contents (accessed 17.04.20). Citizens Advice's *Taking action about harassment*: https://www.citizensadvice.org.uk/law-and-courts/discrimination/taking-action-about-discrimination/taking-action-about-harassment/ (accessed 17.04.20).

12 Working with conflict in social work practice

In the different chapters in this book there has been discussion about how in your social work role you might best go about assessing and dealing with the conflicts that can arise, with particular regard to the rationing of resources, the balancing of the rights and needs of the different people involved in your work, including yourself, and the dual role of care and control inherent in many areas of social work. These issues have been discussed in relation to different service user groups, different settings, between students, and with colleagues, practice educators, tutors, managers and staff in other agencies. It has examined these matters in terms of assessing and managing risks on a personal and agency level, including critical incident analyses (CIAs), and how these can help to reduce the chances of conflict in the future. CIAs can usefully involve a 360-degree examination of what happened from the perspectives of all involved, including service users and carers where possible, or at least trying to imagine it from their viewpoints, taking forward risk assessments and risk management approaches from such an analysis.

The chapters have suggested that there are generic ways of planning for and responding to such conflicts that can be useful to reduce the chances of conflictual behaviours happening, and dealing with them if they do happen. To do this, we have made use of ideas from transactional analysis, the drama triangle and the Johari window in helping to understand, assess and deal with conflicts.

We have considered how service users and carers might be experiencing you in your social work role, using the idea of projective understanding, and how their attributions towards you could lead to conflict or increase the chances of it, or may diminish it, and how you might respond to these attributions and experiences.

Building on the hierarchy of engagement model set out in Chapter 1, and the hierarchy of responses in Chapter 11, we have looked at the types of ways in which we can attempt to work collaboratively with service users and carers, as far as possible making use of openness and honesty as the main approaches where this does not compromise the rights, safety, well-being and safeguarding of service users/carers, or your own. When this is not possible, rationales and strategies have been suggested as to when and why to move on from levels of shared agreement modes to less consensual ones, and how to go about this.

Methods of responding to conflict when it has taken place, such as mediation and relational conflict resolution, which can have a part to play in resolving conflicts more positively, have been set out. Such approaches can achieve discussion of the way the dispute arose and developed, and how best to resolve it, while also helping people learn more personally how to avoid and resolve disputes. These approaches can also be used for example for conflicts between staff, and in team meetings.

If these methods cannot be used or have not worked, then there needs to be a move to ways to protect the most vulnerable, for example between service users, other family members and carers in domestic violence, and in safeguarding children and vulnerable adults in particular.

In order to protect yourself when necessary, there has been examination of what local agency policy, legal and professional bases you can make use of to make demands on managers or practice educators as legislation provides in relation to conflicts arising from aggression, violence, abuse and harassment.

Reflective exercise: your strategies in responding to different types of conflict

From your understandings as a result of what you considered in Chapter 2, in relation to your Parent, Adult and Child ego states, your possible positions on the drama triangle, and the Johari window:

1. How do you, or might you, respond to different types of conflict with service users and/or carers? How might you maintain open and honest communication about key areas and difficult issues, within their possible views of you in your social work role?
2. How might you most appropriately and assertively respond to conflicts with service users, carers, colleagues or managers, and in exchanges with staff in other agencies?
3. Do you need to consider what may prevent you doing what will enable you to recognize and ask for support from your managers/colleagues/ agency? What might you be concerned about, if anything, that might prevent you doing this?

Effective practices and policies

We now look at what should be included in effective policies which would meet the needs of staff and service users given the causes and effects of conflict set out in this book.

Policies should set out to make you:

- feel confident in recognizing risk of conflicts, and feel justified in asking for support, including where violence, threats, harassment or intimidation may affect you or your agency's ability to carry out your work effectively – particularly where this may affect the ability to gain proper access to protect vulnerable children or adults
- feel confident of supportive responses if a situation is building up, or an incident occurs arising from conflictual behaviours
- experience that there is a 'culture of support' in your workplace which makes workers feel secure in the responses of colleagues/managers in the face of potential and actual conflict, violence and/or intimidation, be this with service

users, carers, colleagues, managers, staff in other agencies, or from tutors and/ or practice educators
- aware that there are clear and specific policies concerning the types of support that will be available
- aware of appropriate debriefing if you feel this is needed, possibly independently and in addition to first-line managers' debriefing
- feel there is good clarity in the role and duties of first-line managers, including their role in support processes and supervision
- feel safe with managers and colleagues to work through difficulties arising for you in your work from the type of conflicts addressed in this book
- aware of how triggers for serious conflict are recorded, so that these can be considered in future work: one of the best predictors of behaviours is that they have happened before, and in similar circumstances
- aware that the agency collates reports of violence, threats, harassment or intimidation against staff, prepares action plans to support staff and reduce risks based on these reports, and provides feedback to staff on the outcomes of these processes
- confident that perpetrators will be worked with/responded to on the issues – not necessarily in a punitive way, but in ways which set clear limits and boundaries concerning acceptable behaviour, and make clear the results of breaching them

Conclusion

Within a recognition that conflict can be at the heart of many social work roles, in relation to the dual role of care and control and the balancing of the rights and needs of different people involved where we are intervening, this chapter has suggested ways of considering how we as individuals might best approach such situations. It has also set out what we might ask from employing agencies when we need to carry out work and set limits and boundaries resulting from conflicts, in order to protect not only ourselves, but our service users and carers as well.

References

ACAS (Advisory, Conciliation and Arbitration Service) (undated a) *Tackling race hate incidents in the workplace*. Available at: https://archive.acas.org.uk/racehate (accessed 28.02.20).

ACAS (Advisory, Conciliation and Arbitration Service) (undated b) *Mediation at work*. Available at: https://www.acas.org.uk/mediation (accessed 18.02.20).

ACAS (Advisory, Conciliation and Arbitration Service) (undated c) *Sexual harassment*. Available at: https://www.acas.org.uk/sexual-harassment (accessed 8.04.20).

ACAS (Advisory, Conciliation and Arbitration Service) (2018) *Race Discrimination: Key Points for the Workplace*. London: ACAS. Available at: https://archive.acas.org.uk/media/4413/Race-discrimination-key-points-for-the-workplace/pdf/Race-discrim-keypoints-workplace.pdf (accessed 28.02.20).

Anstiss, B., Polaschek, D.L.L. and Wilson, M. (2011) A brief motivational interviewing intervention with prisoners: when you lead a horse to water, can it drink for itself?, *Psychology, Crime and Law*, 17(8): 689–710.

Bailey, D. (2013) Mental health, in B. Littlechild and R. Smith (eds) *A Handbook for Interprofessional Practice in the Human Services*. Harlow: Pearson, pp. 91–102.

Baron-Cohen, S. (2011) *Zero Degrees of Empathy: A New Theory of Human Cruelty*. London: Penguin.

Barr, H. (2013) Change and challenge in interprofessional education, in B. Littlechild and R. Smith (eds) *A Handbook for Interprofessional Practice in the Human Services*. Harlow: Pearson, pp. 38–49.

Barter, C., Renold, E., Berridge, D. and Cawson, P. (2004) *Peer Violence in Children's Residential Care*. Basingstoke: Palgrave Macmillan.

BASW (British Association of Social Workers) (2012) *The Code of Ethics for Social Work*. Birmingham: BASW. Available at: https://www.basw.co.uk/about-basw/code-ethics (accessed 2.03.20).

BASW (British Association of Social Workers) (2014) *BASW Whistleblowing Policy*. Available at: https://www.basw.co.uk/resources/basw-whistleblowing-policy (accessed 2.03.20).

BASW (British Association of Social Workers) (2018a) *Insult and Injury: Exploring the Impacts of Intimidation, Threats and Violence against Social Workers*. Belfast: BASW.

BASW (British Association of Social Workers) (2018b) *Professional Capabilities Framework: end of first placement*. Available at: https://www.basw.co.uk/professional-development/professional-capabilities-framework-pcf/the-pcf/first-placement (accessed 2.03.20).

BASWO, Welsh Government (2018a) *Domestic abuse from a BME perspective*. Available at http://www.bawso.org.uk/home/what-is-domestic-abuse/domestic-abuse-from-a-bme-perspective/ (accessed 2.03.20).

BASWO, Welsh Government (2018b) *Domestic abuse*. Available at https://gov.wales/live-fear-free/domestic-abuse-wales (accessed 2.03.20).

Ben-Ari, A. and Strier, R. (2010) Rethinking cultural competence: what can we learn from Levinas?, *British Journal of Social Work*, 40(7): 2155–67.

Beresford, P. (2012) What service users want from social workers, *Community Care* website. Available at: https://www.communitycare.co.uk/2012/04/27/what-service-users-want-from-social-workers/ (accessed 18.02.20).

Berkman, C.S. and Zinberg, G. (1997) Homophobia and heterosexism in social workers, *Social Work*, 42(4): 319–32.

Bernard, C., Fairtlough, A., Fletcher, J. and Ahmet, A. (2014) A qualitative study of marginalised social work students' views of social work education and learning, *British Journal of Social Work*, 44(7): 1934–49.

Berne, E. (1964) *Games People Play: The Basic Handbook of Transactional Analysis*. New York: Ballantine Books.

Biehal, N., Cusworth, L., Wade, J. with Clarke, S. (2014) *Keeping Children Safe: Allegations Concerning the Abuse or Neglect of Children in Care: Final Report*. London: NSPCC. Available at: https://learning.nspcc.org.uk/children-and-families-at-risk/looked-after-children/#heading-top (accessed 2.03.20).

Black, M.C. (2011) Intimate partner violence and adverse health consequences: implications for clinicians, *American Journal of Lifestyle Medicine*, 5(5): 428–39.

Boud, D. and Feletti, G. (2013) *The Challenge of Problem-Based Learning*. London: Routledge.

Brandon, M., Bailey, S., Belderson, P. et al. (2009) *Understanding Serious Case Reviews and their Impact: A Biennial Analysis of Serious Case Reviews 2005–07*. London: Department for Children, Schools and Families.

Brandon, M., Sidebotham, P., Bailey, S. et al. (2012) *New Learning from Serious Case Reviews: A Two-Year Report for 2009–11*. London: Department for Education.

Brigley Thompson, Z. (2018) From safe spaces to precarious moments: teaching sexuality and violence in the American higher education classroom, *Gender and Education*, 32(3): 395–411. DOI: 10.1080/09540253.2018.1458077.

Bubar, R., Cespedes, K., and Bundy-Fazioli, K. (2016) Intersectionality and social work: omissions of race, class, and sexuality in graduate school education, *Journal of Social Work Education*, 52(3): 283–96.

Burgess, R.C. (2005) A model for enhancing individual and organisational learning of 'emotional intelligence': the drama and winner's triangles, *Social Work Education*, 24(1): 97–112. DOI: 10.1080/0261547052000325008.

Byers, C. and Creating Links (2013) Member of the team? Carers' experiences of interprofessional working: key issues in current policy and practice, in B. Littlechild and R. Smith (eds) *A Handbook for Interprofessional Practice in the Human Services*. Harlow: Pearson, pp. 200–14.

Caller, R. (2013) Why mediation is key to helping social workers resolve best interests disputes, *Community Care* website. Available at: https://www.communitycare.co.uk/2013/09/02/why-mediation-is-key-to-helping-social-workers-resolve-best-interests-disputes/ (accessed 18.02.20).

Carr, H. and Goosey, D. (2017) *Law for Social Workers*. Oxford: Oxford University Press.

Carthy, A. and McGilloway, S. (2015) 'Thinking outside the box': promoting learning through emotional and social skills development, *Procedia – Social and Behavioural Sciences*, 191: 2655–60.

Chief Social Worker for England (2014) *Knowledge and skills for child and family social work*. Available at: http://traininginpractice.co.uk/knowledge-and-skills-for-child/ and https://assets.publishing.service.gov.uk/government/uploads/system/uploads/attachment_data/file/338718/140730_Knowledge_and_skills_statement_final_version_AS_RH_Checked.pdf (accessed 24.04.20).

Child Poverty Action Group (2019) *Child poverty facts and figures*. Available at: https://cpag.org.uk/child-poverty/child-poverty-facts-and-figures (accessed 24.04. 20).

Chinnell, J. (2011) Three voices: reflections on homophobia and heterosexism in social work education, *Social Work Education*, 30(7): 759–73.

Chonody, J., Woodford, M.R., Smith, S. and Silverschanz, P. (2013) Christian social work students' attitudes toward lesbians and gay men: religious teachings, religiosity and contact, *Journal of Religion and Spirituality in Social Work, Social Thought*, 32(3): 211–26.

CIPD (Chartered Institute of Personnel and Development) (undated) *Bullying and harassment.* Available at: https://www.cipd.co.uk/news-views/viewpoint/bullying-harassment (accessed 24.04.20).

Clement, B. (1996) Social worker wins £175,000 for breakdowns: stress at work: ruling could open floodgates, *Independent,* 27 April. Available at: https://www.independent.co.uk/news/social-worker-wins-pounds-175000-for-breakdowns-1306944.html (accessed 2.03.20).

Clouston, T.J., Westcott, L., Whitcombe, S.W., Riley, J. and Matheson, R. (eds) (2010) *Problem-Based Learning in Health and Social Care.* Hoboken, NJ: John Wiley & Sons.

Community Care (2010) *Fifth of staff who have suffered violence work in social care.* Available at: https://www.communitycare.co.uk/2010/11/19/fifth-of-staff-who-have-suffered-violence-work-in-social-care/ (accessed 24.04.20).

Community Care (2011) *Social workers struggle with hostile and intimidating parents.* Available at: https://www.communitycare.co.uk/2011/09/30/social-workers-struggle-with-hostile-and-intimidating-parents/ (accessed 2.03.20).

Community Care (2014) *85% of social workers were assaulted, harassed or verbally abused in the past year.* Available at: https://www.communitycare.co.uk/2014/09/16/violence-social-workers-just-part-job-70-incidents-investigated/ (accessed 24.04.20).

Cooper, J. (2011) Most social workers threatened in past six months, *Community Care* website. Available at: http://www.communitycare.co.uk/2011/11/14/most-social-workers-threatened-in-past-six-months/#.UnNkoUT2hlA (accessed 2.03.20).

Cornes, M. (2013) Older people, in B. Littlechild and R. Smith (eds) *A Handbook for Interprofessional Practice in the Human Services.* Harlow: Pearson, pp. 143–58.

Coulshed V. and Orme, J. (2006) *Social Work Practice,* 4th edn. BASW Practical Social Work series. Basingstoke: Palgrave Macmillan.

Creating Links (2019) 'Creating links': the involvement of service users and carers in the provision of social work education in England, in M. Granosik, A. Gulczyńska, M. Kostrzyńska and B. Littlechild (eds) *Participatory Social Work: Research, Practice, Education.* Kraków: Jagiellonian University Press. Łódź University Press and Jagiellonian University Press, Łódź–Kraków.

Cree, V.E. and Davis, A. (2007) *Voices from the Inside.* London: Routledge.

Crown Prosecution Service (undated) *Honour based violence and forced marriage.* Available at: https://www.cps.gov.uk/publication/honour-based-violence-and-forced-marriage (accessed 16.02.20).

Culwick, M. and Wallace, C. (2013) Learning disabilities, in B. Littlechild and R. Smith (eds) *A Handbook for Interprofessional Practice in the Human Services.* Harlow: Pearson, pp. 103–16.

De Waal, F.B. and Luttrell, L.M. (1986) The similarity principle underlying social bonding among female rhesus monkeys, *Folia Primatologica,* 46(4): 215–34.

Denney, D. (2010) Violence and social care staff: positive and negative approaches to risk, *British Journal of Social Work,* 40(4): 1297–313.

Dentato, M.P., Craig, S.L., Lloyd, M.R., Kelly, B.L., Wright, C. and Austin, A. (2016) Homophobia within schools of social work: the critical need for affirming classroom settings and effective preparation for service with the LGBTQ community, *Social Work Education,* 35(6): 672–92.

Department for Education (2018a) *Information sharing advice for safeguarding practitioners: Guidance on information sharing for people who provide safeguarding services to children, young people, parents and carers.* Available at: https://www.gov.uk/government/publications/safeguarding-practitioners-information-sharing-advice (accessed 2.03.20).

Department for Education (2018b) *Post-Qualifying Standard: Knowledge and Skills Statement for Child and Family Practitioners.* London: Department for Education. Available at: https://assets.publishing.service.gov.uk/government/uploads/system/uploads/attachment_data/file/708704/Post-qualifying_standard-KSS_for_child_and_family_practitioners.pdf (accessed 2.03.20).

Department of Health (2011) *Adult safeguarding: statement of government policy.* Available at: https://www.gov.uk/government/publications/adult-safeguarding-statement-of-government-policy (accessed 26.02.20).

Department of Health (2015) *Knowledge and Skills Statement for Social Workers in Adult Services.* London: Department for Education. Available at: https://assets.publishing.service.gov.uk/government/uploads/system/uploads/attachment_data/file/411957/KSS.pdf (accessed 2.03.20).

Department of Health and Social Care (2016) *Care Act 2014: supporting implementation: support for local authorities to carry out the implementation for part 1 of the Care Act 2014.* Available at: https://www.gov.uk/government/publications/care-act-statutory-guidance (accessed 26.02.20).

Dessel, A., Bolen, R. and Shepardson, C. (2011) Can religious expression and sexual orientation affirmation coexist in social work? A critique of Hodge's theoretical, theological, and conceptual frameworks, *Journal of Social Work Education*, 47(2): 213–34.

Devore, W. and Schlezinger, E.C. (1981) *Ethnic-Sensitive Social Work Practice.* St Louis: CV Mosby.

Dewane, J. (2015) Solution-focused supervision: a go-to approach, *Social Work Today*, 15(5): 24. Available at: https://www.socialworktoday.com/archive/090915p24.shtml (accessed 2.03.20).

Dingwall, D., Eekelaar, J. and Murray, T. (1983) *The Protection of Children: State Intervention and Family Life.* Oxford: Basil Blackwell.

Dingwall, D., Eekelaar, J. and Murray, T. (2014) *The Protection of Children: State Intervention and Family Life*, 2nd edn. New Orleans: Quid Pro Books.

Donaldson, G. (2009) What can physiotherapists learn from disabled people's experiences of rehabilitation using a social model perspective? MPhil thesis submitted to Lancaster University, Lancaster.

Donaldson, G. and Sapey, B. (2013) Rehabilitation and disabled people, in B. Littlechild and R. Smith (eds) *A Handbook for Interprofessional Practice in the Human Services.* Harlow: Pearson, pp. 171–84.

Donati, P. and Archer, M.S. (2015) *The Relational Subject.* Cambridge: Cambridge University Press.

Donovan, C., Hester, M., Holmes, J. and McCarry, M. (2006) *Comparing domestic abuse in same sex and heterosexual relationships.* Available at: http://www.bristol.ac.uk/media-library/sites/sps/migrated/documents/rc1307finalreport.pdf (accessed 2.03.20).

Duhigg, C. (2016) What Google learned from its quest to build the perfect team, *New York Times Magazine*, 25 February. Available at: https://www.nytimes.com/2016/02/28/magazine/what-google-learned-from-its-quest-to-build-the-perfect-team.html (accessed 14.08.19).

Emerson, E. (1995) *Challenging Behaviour: Analysis and Intervention in People with Learning Disabilities.* Cambridge: Cambridge University Press.

Emerson, S. (1996) Creating a safe place for growth in supervision, *Contemporary Family Therapy*, 18(3): 393–403.

Eraut, M. (1998) Concepts of competence, *Journal of Interprofessional Care*, 12(2): 127–39.

ESRC Centre on Dynamics of Ethnicity (CoDE) (2013) *Ethnicity and Deprivation in England: How Likely are Ethnic Minorities to Live in Deprived Neighbourhoods?* Manchester: University of Manchester/Joseph Rowntree Foundation. Available at: http://hummedia.manchester.ac.uk/institutes/code/briefingsupdated/ethnicity-and-deprivation-in-england-how-likely-are-ethnic-minorities-to-live-in-deprived-neighbourhoods%20(1).pdf (accessed 24.04.20).

Fauth, B., Jelicic, H., Hart, D. et al. (2010) *Effective Practice to Protect Children Living in 'Highly Resistant' Families.* London: Centre for Excellence and Outcomes in Children and Young People's Services (C4EO). Available at: https://www.bl.uk/collection-items/effective-practice-to-protect-children-living-in-highly-resistant-families (accessed 2.03.20).

Featherstone, B., Morris, K. and White, S. (2014a) A marriage made in hell: early intervention meets child protection, *British Journal of Social Work*, 44(7): 1735–49.

Featherstone, B., White, S. and Morris, K. (2014b) *Re-Imagining Child Protection: Towards Humane Social Work with Families*. Bristol: Policy Press.

Fernando, T. and Bennett, B. (2019) Creating a culturally safe space when teaching Aboriginal content in social work: a scoping review, *Australian Social Work*, 72(1): 47–61.

Forrester, D., Westlake, D. and Glynn, G. (2012) Parental resistance and social worker skills: towards a theory of motivational social work, *Child and Family Social Work*, 17(2): 118–29.

Freire, P. (1996) *Pedagogy of the Oppressed*, revised edn. New York: Continuum.

Frost, N. (2013) Children in need, looked-after children and interprofessional working, in B. Littlechild and R. Smith (eds) *A Handbook for Interprofessional Practice in the Human Services*. Harlow: Pearson, pp. 131–42.

Gerdes, K.E. and Segal, E. (2011) Importance of empathy for social work practice: integrating new science, *Social Work*, 56(2): 141–8.

Gilbert, P. (2005) Compassion and cruelty: a biopsychosocial approach, in P. Gilbert (ed.) *Compassion: Conceptualisations, Research and Use in Psychotherapy*. New York: Routledge, pp. 9–74.

Gilbert, T. (2016) Embedding and assessing compassion in the university curriculum, in *The European Conference on Education 2016: Official Conference Proceedings*. Brighton: International Academic Forum, pp.77–88.

Gilbert, T. (2017) When looking is allowed: what compassionate group work looks like in a UK university, in P. Gibbs (ed.) *The Pedagogy of Compassion at the Heart of Higher Education*. Cham, Switzerland: Springer International Publishing.

Gilbert, T. (2019) Telephone call with Rose Parkes, 30 July 2019.

Gilbert, T., Doolan, M., Beka, S., Spencer, N, Crotta, M. and Davari, S. (2018) Compassion on university degree programmes at a UK university: the neuroscience of effective groupwork, *Journal of Research in Innovative Teaching and Learning*, 11(1): 4–21.

Goodman-Brown, T.B., Edelstein, R.S., Goodman, G.S., Jones, D.P.H. and Gordon, D.S. (2003) Why children tell: a model of children's disclosure of sexual abuse, *Child Abuse and Neglect*, 27(5): 525–40.

Government Equalities Office (2010) Guidance Equality Act 2010: Information and guidance on the Equality Act 2010, including age discrimination and public sector Equality Duty, gov.uk. Available at: https://www.gov.uk/guidance/equality-act-2010-guidance (accessed 2.03.20).

Gov.uk (undated a) Public Interest Disclosure Act 1998. Available at: https://www.legislation.gov.uk/ukpga/1998/23/section/1 (accessed 3.03.20).

Gov.uk (undated b) *Whistleblowing for employees*. Available at: https://www.gov.uk/whistleblowing/how-to-blow-the-whistle (accessed 3.03.20).

Gov.uk (2015) *Francis Report: update and response*. Available at: https://www.gov.uk/government/speeches/francis-report-update-and-response (accessed 24.04.20).

Gov.uk (2017) *Lammy review: final report: An independent review into the treatment of, and outcomes for Black, Asian and Minority Ethnic individuals in the criminal justice system*. Available at: https://www.gov.uk/government/publications/lammy-review-final-report (accessed 28.02.20).

Grierson, J. (2017) Christian thrown out of university over anti-gay remarks loses appeal, *Guardian*, 27 October. Available at: https://www.theguardian.com/uk-news/2017/oct/27/christian-felix-ngole-thrown-out-sheffield-university-anti-gay-remarks-loses-appeal (accessed 23.01.19).

Hall, D. (2003) Child protection – lessons from Victoria Climbié, *BMJ*, 326(7384): 293–4.

Harris, T. (2004) *I'm OK – You're OK: A Practical Guide to Transactional Analysis*. New York: Harper.

Hawley, H., Littlechild, B., Sivakumaran, T., Sender, H., Gale, T.M. and Wilson, K.J. (2006) Structure and content of risk assessment proformas in mental healthcare, *Journal of Mental Health*, 15(4): 437–48.

HCPC (Health and Care Professions Council) (2015) *The Fitness to Practise Process*. London: HCPC.

HCPC (Health and Care Professions Council) (2016) *Guidance on Conduct and Ethics for Students*. London: HCPC.

HCPC (Health and Care Professions Council) (2017) *Standards of Proficiency: Social Workers in England*. London: HCPC. Available at: https://www.local.gov.uk/sites/default/files/documents/standards-proficiency-soc-906.pdf (accessed 24.02.20).

Healy, L. (2007) Universalism and cultural relativism in social work ethics, *International Social Work*, 50(1): 11–26. Available at: http://isw.sagepub.com/cgi/content/abstract/50/1/11 (accessed 2.03.20).

Hester, M. (2013) Who does what to whom? Gender and domestic violence perpetrators in English police records, *European Journal of Criminology*, 10: 623–37.

Hester, M. and Westmarland, N. (2005) *Tackling Domestic Violence: Effective Interventions and Approaches*. London: Home Office Research, Development and Statistics Directorate.

Higashida, N. (2013) *The Reason I Jump: One Boy's Voice from the Silence of Autism*. London: Sceptre Books.

HM Government (1989) Children Act 1989. Available at: http://www.legislation.gov.uk/ukpga/1989/41/contents (accessed 2.03.20).

HM Government (2018) *Working Together to Safeguard Children: A Guide to Inter-Agency Working to Safeguard and Promote the Welfare of Children*. London: HM Government. Available at: https://assets.publishing.service.gov.uk/government/uploads/system/uploads/attachment_data/file/779401/Working_Together_to_Safeguard-Children.pdf (accessed 2.03.20).

Hodge, D.R. (2013) Moving toward a more inclusive educational environment? A multi-sample exploration of religious discrimination as seen through the eyes of students from various faith traditions, *Journal of Social Work Education*, 42(2): 249–67.

Holley, L.C. and Steiner, S. (2005) Safe space: student perspectives on classroom environment, *Journal of Social Work Education*, 41(1): 49–64.

Home Office (2014) *Working together to safeguard children: Multi-Agency Safeguarding Hubs*. Available at: https://www.gov.uk/government/news/working-together-to-safeguard-children-multi-agency-safeguarding-hubs (accessed 2.03.20).

Home Office (2015) *Controlling or Coercive Behaviour in an Intimate or Family Relationship: Statutory Guidance Framework*. London: Home Office. Available at: https://assets.publishing.service.gov.uk/government/uploads/system/uploads/attachment_data/file/482528/Controlling_or_coercive_behaviour_-_statutory_guidance.pdf (accessed 1.03.20).

Home Office and Department of Health (2015) *No secrets: guidance on protecting vulnerable adults in care*. Available at: https://www.gov.uk/government/publications/no-secrets-guidance-on-protecting-vulnerable-adults-in-care (accessed 24.04.20).

Howe, D. (2008) *The Emotionally Intelligent Social Worker*. London: Red Globe Press.

Human Rights Act 1998 (c.42). London: HMSO. Available at: http://www.legislation.gov.uk/ukpga/1998/42/schedule/1/part/I/chapter/8 (accessed 5.10.19).

Humphreys, C. and Stanley, N. (2006) *Domestic Violence and Child Protection: Directions for Good Practice*. London: Jessica Kingsley Publishers.

Hunt, S., Goddard, C., Cooper, J., Littlechild, B. and Wild, J. (2016) 'If I feel like this, how does the child feel?' Child protection workers, supervision, management and organisational responses to parental violence, *Journal of Social Work Practice: Psychotherapeutic Approaches in Health, Welfare and the Community*, 30(1): 5–24. Published online 14 September 2015.

Hylton, M.E. (2005) Heteronormativity and the experiences of lesbian and bisexual women as social work students, *Journal of Social Work Education*, 41(1): 67–82.

IFSW (International Federation of Social Workers) (2014) *Global definition of social work*. Rheinfelden, Switzerland: IFSW. Available at: https://www.ifsw.org/what-is-social-work/global-definition-of-social-work/ (accessed 20.08.19).

Johnson, P., Kelly, E., Lee, T. et al. (2018) *Securing the future: funding health and social care to the 2030s*, Health Foundation and the Institute for Fiscal Studies. Available at: https://www.ifs.org.uk/publications/12994 (accessed 18.02.20).

Jude, J. (2018) The practice of systemic reflexivity, *Journal of Social Work Practice*, 32(1): 45–57. DOI: 10.1080/02650533.2017.1291499.

Kagan, M., Orkibi, E. and Zychlinski, E. (2017) 'Wicked', 'deceptive', and 'blood sucking': cyberbullying against social workers in Israel as claims-making activity, *Qualitative Social Work*, 17(6): 778–94.

Kalina, C. and Powell, K. (2009) Cognitive and social constructivism: developing tools for an effective classroom, *Education*, 130(2): 241–50.

King, M., Semlyen, J., Tai, S.S. et al. (2008) A systematic review of mental disorder, suicide, and deliberate self-harm in lesbian, gay and bisexual people, *BMC Psychiatry*, 8(70): 1–17. DOI: 10.1186/1471-244X-8-70.

Kisfalvi, V. and Oliver, D. (2015) Creating and maintaining a safe space in experiential learning, *Journal of Management Education*, 39(6): 713–40.

Kline, R. with Khan, S. (2013) The Duty of Care of Healthcare Professionals: Practical advice on the duty of care of healthcare professionals and their employers and what we must do to help protect patients and staff. London: Public World. Available at: http://www.publicworld.org/files/Duty_of_Care_handbook_April_2013.pdf (accessed 2.03.20).

Kolb, D.A. (2014) Experiential learning: experience as the source of learning and development, 2nd edn. Upper Saddle River, NJ: Pearson Education.

Langan, J. (2000) The risk factor, *Professional Social Work*, 9 February.

Langan, J. and Lindow, V. (2004) *Living with the Risk: Mental Health Service User Involvement in Risk Assessment and Management*. Bristol: Joseph Rowntree Foundation/Policy Press.

LankellyChase Foundation (2014) *Ethnic Inequalities in Mental Health: Promoting Lasting Positive Change: Report of Findings to LankellyChase Foundation, Mind, The Afiya Trust and Centre for Mental Health*. Available at: https://lankellychase.org.uk/wp-content/uploads/2015/07/Ethnic-Inequality-in-Mental-Health-Confluence-Full-Report-March2014.pdf (accessed 28.02.20).

Leyerzapf, H., Visse, M., De Beer, A. and Abma, T.A. (2018) Gay-friendly elderly care: creating space for sexual diversity in residential care by challenging the hetero norm, *Ageing and Society*, 38(2): 352–77.

Littlechild, B. (1997) *Dealing with Aggression*. Birmingham: Venture Press.

Littlechild, B. (2002) *The Management of Conflict and Service User Violence against Child-Protection Social Staff in Hertfordshire*. Hatfield: Centre for Community Research, University of Hertfordshire.

Littlechild, B. (2003) *An Evaluation of the Implementation of a Restorative Justice Approach in a Residential Unit for Young People in Hertfordshire*. Hatfield: University of Hertfordshire.

Littlechild, B. (2005) The nature and effects of violence against child-protection social workers: providing effective support, *British Journal of Social Work*, 35(3): 387–401.

Littlechild, B. (2009) Restorative justice, mediation and relational conflict resolution in work with young people in residential care, *Practice: Social Work in Action*, 21(6): 229–40.

Littlechild, B. (2010) Conflict resolution, restorative justice approaches and bullying in young people's residential units, *Children and Society*, (25)1: 47–58.

Littlechild, B. (2012) Values and cultural issues in social work, *European Research Institute for Social Work web journal*, 1/2012. Available at: http://periodika.osu.cz/eris/dok/2012-01/07_values_and_cultural_issues_in_sw.pdf (accessed 2.03.20).

Littlechild, B. and Hawley, C. (2010) Risk assessments for mental health service users: ethical, valid and reliable?, *Journal of Social Work*, 10(2): 211–29.

Littlechild, B., Hunt, S., Goddard, C., Cooper, J., Raynes, B. and Wild, J. (2016) The effects of violence and aggression from parents on child protection workers' personal, family and professional lives, *Sage Open*, 6(1): 1–12. DOI: 10.1177/2158244015624951.

Lord Laming (2003) *The Victoria Climbié Inquiry: Report of an Inquiry by Lord Laming*. London: Stationery Office.

Lubker, D.K.V. (2004) Socioeconomic status and domestic violence, *International Journal of Global Health and Health Disparities*, 3(1): 85–91. Available at: http://scholarworks.uni.edu/ijghhd/vol3/iss1/10 (accessed 2.03.20).

Lymbery, M. (2010) A new vision for adult social care: continuities and change in the care of older people, *Critical Social Policy*, 30(1): 5–26.

Lyons, N. (2010) *Handbook of Reflection and Reflective Inquiry: Mapping a Way of Knowing for Professional Reflective Inquiry*. New York: Springer.

Mathews, I., Simpson, D., and Crawford, K. (2013) *Your Social Work Practice Placement: From Start to Finish*. London: Sage Publications.

Mattsson, T. (2013) Intersectionality as a useful tool: anti-oppressive social work and critical reflection, *Affilia*, 29(1): 8–17.

McElvaney, R. (2003) Disclosure of child sexual abuse: delays, non-disclosure and partial disclosure. What the research tells us and implications for practice, *Child Abuse Review*, 24(3):159–69. Available at: https://onlinelibrary.wiley.com/doi/full/10.1002/car.2280?casa_token=zvtOaGtHDi4AAAAA%3AkvYNXTtFdhFvtuY-zNi0FCry5CvhAEEOmL-A_zpQmJKcHGP0ZaxoRfxFtN538MHB_fR0dt0oxX2vF38 (accessed 2.03.20).

McGrath M. (1991) *Multidisciplinary Teamwork*. Aldershot: Avebury.

McLaughlin, H. (2013) Keeping interprofessional practice honest: fads and critical reflections, in B. Littlechild and R. Smith (eds) *A Handbook for Interprofessional Practice in the Human Services*. Harlow: Pearson, pp. 50–61.

Megele, C. (2015) *Psychosocial and Relationship-Based Practice*. Northwich: Critical Publishing.

Meltzer, H., Doos, L., Vostanis, P., Ford, T. and Goodman, R. (2009) The mental health of children who witness domestic violence, *Child and Family Social Work*, 14(4): 491–501.

Melville-Wiseman, J. (2013) Teaching through the tension: resolving religious and sexuality based schism in social work education, *International Social Work*, 56(3): 290–309.

Mental Health Taskforce (2016) *The Five Year Forward View For Mental Health: A Report from the Independent Mental Health Taskforce to the NHS in England*. Leeds: NHS England. Available at: https://www.england.nhs.uk/wp-content/uploads/2016/02/Mental-Health-Taskforce-FYFV-final.pdf (accessed 2.03.20).

Milner, J. and O'Byrne, P. (2002) *Assessment in Social Work*. Basingstoke: Palgrave.

Morrison, T. (2007) Emotional intelligence, emotion and social work: context, characteristics, complications and contribution, *British Journal of Social Work*, 37(2): 245–63.

Morton, J., Jeyasingham, D. and Hicks, S. (2013) The social work of sexuality: rethinking approaches to social work education, *Health and Social Care Education*, 2(2): 16–19.

National Autistic Society (undated) *Autism*. Available at: https://www.autism.org.uk/about/what-is/asd.aspx (accessed 2.03.20).

Neff, K. (2003) Self-compassion: an alternative conceptualization of a healthy attitude toward oneself, *Self and Identity*, 2(2): 85–101.

Newman, B.S., Dannenfelser, P.L. and Benishek, L. (2002) Assessing beginning social work and counseling students' acceptance of lesbians and gay men, *Journal of Social Work Education*, 38(2): 273–88.

NHS (2018) *Abuse and neglect of vulnerable adults*. Available at: https://www.nhs.uk/conditions/social-care-and-support-guide/help-from-social-services-and-charities/abuse-and-neglect-vulnerable-adults/ (accessed 2.03.20).

NHS Nottingham University Hospitals Trust (undated) *Caldicott Guardian*. Available at: https://www.nuh.nhs.uk/caldicott-guardian (accessed 2.03.20).

NICE (National Institute for Health and Care Excellence) (2014) *Domestic Violence and Abuse: Multi-Agency Working: Public Health Guideline*. London: NICE. Available at: https://www.nice.org.uk/guidance/ph50/resources/domestic-violence-and-abuse-multiagency-working-pdf-1996411687621 (accessed 2.03.20).

NICE (National Institute for Health and Care Excellence) (2015a) *Challenging behaviour and learning disabilities: prevention and interventions for people with learning disabilities whose behaviour challenges*. Available at: https://www.nice.org.uk/guidance/ng11 (accessed 2.03.20).

NICE (National Institute for Health and Care Excellence) (2015b) *Violence and aggression: short-term management in mental health, health and community settings*. Available at: https://www.nice.org.uk/guidance/ng10 (accessed 2.03.20).

NICE (National Institute for Health and Care Excellence) (2018a) *Domestic violence and abuse*. Available at: https://cks.nice.org.uk/domestic-violence-and-abuse#!scenario (accessed 2.03.20).

NICE (National Institute for Health and Care Excellence) (2018b) *Learning disabilities and behaviour that challenges: service design and delivery NICE guideline [NG93]*. Available at: https://www.nice.org.uk/guidance/ng93 (accessed 2.03.20).

Nixon, J. and Humphreys, C. (2010) Marshalling the evidence: using intersectionality in the domestic violence frame, *Social Politics: International Studies in Gender, State and Society*, 17(2): 137–58. Available at: https://doi.org/10.1093/sp/jxq003 (accessed 2.03.20).

NSPCC (2014) *Culture and faith: learning from case reviews: summary of risk factors and learning for improved practice around culture and faith*. Available at: https://learning.nspcc.org.uk/research-resources/learning-from-case-reviews/culture-faith/ (accessed 2.03.20).

O'Brien, J. (1987) A guide to personal futures planning, in G. Bellamy and B. Wilcox (eds) *A Comprehensive Guide to the Activities Catalogue: An Alternative Curriculum for Youth and Adults with Severe Disabilities*. Baltimore, MD: Paul H. Brooks.

Office for National Statistics (2018) *Women most at risk of experiencing partner abuse in England and Wales: years ending March 2015 to 2017*. Available at: https://www.ons.gov.uk/peoplepopulationandcommunity/crimeandjustice/articles/womenmostatriskofexperiencingpartnerabuseinenglandandwales/yearsendingmarch2015to2017 (accessed 18.02.20).

Office for Students (2020) *Freedom of speech*. Available at: https://www.officeforstudents.org.uk/advice-and-guidance/student-wellbeing-and-protection/freedom-of-speech/ (accessed 18.02.20).

O'Hara, A. (2011) Understanding and managing conflict, in A. O'Hara and R. Pockett (eds) *Skills for Human Service Practice*, 2nd edn. Oxford: Oxford University Press, pp. 209–24.

Page-Gould, E., Mendoza-Denton, R. and Tropp, L.R. (2008) With a little help from my cross-group friend: reducing anxiety in intergroup contexts through cross-group friendship, *Journal of Personality and Social Psychology*, 95(5): 1080–94.

Parton, N. (2010) Child protection and safeguarding in England: changing and competing conceptions of risk and their implications for social work, *British Journal of Social Work*, 41(5): 854–75.

Parton, N. (2014) Social work, child protection and politics: some critical and constructive reflections, *British Journal of Social Work*, 44(7): 2042–56.

Pattoni, P. (2012) Strengths-based approaches for working with individuals, *Iriss* website. Available at: https://www.iriss.org.uk/resources/insights/strengths-based-approaches-working-individuals (accessed 28.2.20).

Payne, M. (2014) *Modern Social Work Theory*, 4th edn. *Basingstoke: Palgrave Macmillan.*

Piaget, J. and Cook, M. (1952) *The Origins of Intelligence in Children*. New York: International Universities Press.

Pitman, E. (1982) Transactional analysis: an introduction to its theory and practice, *British Journal of Social Work*, 12(1): 47–63.

Pitman, E. (1990) *Transactional Analysis for Social Workers and Counsellors: An Introduction*. Oxon: Routledge & Kegan Paul.

Powell, J.A. and Menendian, S. (2016) The problem of othering: towards inclusiveness and belonging, *Othering and Belonging*, 1: 14–39.

Redmond, M. (2010) Safe space oddity: revisiting critical pedagogy, *Journal of Teaching in Social Work*, 30(1): 1–14.

Rees, C.A. (2006) The care of looked-after children, *Current Paediatrics*, 16(2): 83–90.

Reid, W.J. and Epstein L. (eds) (1972) *Task-Centred Casework*. New York: Colombia University Press.

Ruch, G. (2012) Where have all the feelings gone? Developing reflective and relationship-based management in child-care social work, *British Journal of Social Work*, 42(7): 1315–32.

Sellman, D. (2010) Values and ethics in interprofessional working, in K.C. Pollard, J. Thomas and M. Miers (eds) *Understanding Interprofessional Working in Health and Social Care: Theory and Practice*. Basingstoke: Palgrave Macmillan, pp. 156–70.

Sheldon, B. and MacDonald, G. (2009) *A Textbook of Social Work*. London: Routledge.

Siddique, H. (2012) Wales child abuse scandal: key questions answered, *Guardian*, 6 November. Available at: https://www.theguardian.com/society/2012/nov/06/wales-child-abuse-scandal-questions (accessed 3.03.20).

Singh, G. and Cowden, S. (2013) Is cultural sensitivity always a good thing? Arguments for a universalist social work, in M. Carey and L. Green (eds) *Practical Social Work Ethics: Complex Dilemmas Within Applied Social Care*. Farnham: Ashgate, pp. 63–82.

Skills for Care (undated a) *Johari window: populated example of use at social worker level of the PCF*. Available at: https://www.skillsforcare.org.uk/Document-library/Social-work/Measuring-impact/Populated-johari-window.pdf (accessed 28.2.20).

Skills for Care (undated b) *Work Smart, Work Safe: Combating Violence Against Care Staff*. Leeds: Skills for Care. Available at: https://www.skillsforcare.org.uk/Document-library/Standards/Safety-guidance/Work%20smart,%20work%20safe%20-%20guide%20for%20employers.pdf (accessed 28.02.20).

Skills for Care (2013) *Violence Against Social Care and Support Staff: Summary of Research*. Leeds: Skills for Care. Available at: https://www.skillsforcare.org.uk/Document-library/NMDS-SC,-workforce-intelligence-and-innovation/Research/Violence-reports/Violence-against-social-care-workers---composite-report.pdf (accessed 24.04.20).

Smith, K., Flatley, J., Coleman, K. et al. (eds) (2010) *Homicides, Firearm Offences and Intimate Violence 2008/09*, supplementary volume 2 to *Crime in England and Wales 2008/09*, 3rd edn. London: Home Office.

Smith, R. (2013) The drivers and dynamics of interprofessional working in policy and practice, in B. Littlechild and R. Smith (eds) *A Handbook for Interprofessional Practice in the Human Services*. Harlow: Pearson, pp. 24–37.

Social Work England (2019a) *Professional standards*. Available at: https://socialworkengland.org.uk/professional-standards/ (accessed 2.03.20).

Social Work England (2019b) *Qualifying education and training standards 2020 guidance*. Available at: https://www.socialworkengland.org.uk/standards/guidance-documents/qualifying-education-and-training-standards-guidance/ (accessed 10.02.20).

Stone, C. (2016) The role of practice educators in initial and post qualifying social worker education, *Social Work Education*, 35(6): 706–18. DOI: 10.1080/02615479.2016.1185407.

Stonewall, (undated) *Harassment in the workplace: understanding and spotting harassment in the workplace for LGBT people, and what the law says*. Available at: https://www.stonewall.org.uk/harassment-workplace (accessed 28.02.20).

Swank, E. and Raiz, L. (2010) Attitudes towards gays and lesbians among undergraduate social work students, *Journal of Women and Social Work*, 25(1): 9–29.

TCSW (The College of Social Work) (2012) *Practice Learning Guidance: Overview of New Arrangements for Practice Learning*. London: TCSW. Available at: https://aru.ac.uk/-/media/Files/NHS-Mentors/Social-Work-(FHSCE)/Useful-weblinks/TCSW-overview-of-new-arrangements-for-practice-learning.pdf?la=en&hash=60923EB929374C589F67737F81B6015B (accessed 23.04.20).

Tes (1995) *Walker v Northumberland County Council 1995*. Available at: https://www.tes.com/teaching-resource/walker-v-northumberland-county-council-1995-11334641 (accessed 4.03.20).

The Stationery Office (2000) *Lost in Care – Report of the Tribunal of Inquiry into the Abuse of Children in the Former County Council Areas of Gwynedd and Clwyd since 1974*. London: The Stationery Office. Available at: http://www.julyseventh.co.uk/pdf/Lost_In_Care_Report-Formatted.pdf (accessed 3.03.20).

Thiara, R. and Breslin, R. (2006) A look at domestic violence among families from ethnic minorities, *Community Care* website. Available at: https://www.communitycare.co.uk/2006/11/01/a-look-at-domestic-violence-among-families-from-ethnic-minorities/ (accessed 2.03.20).

Thompson, N. (2001) *Anti-Discriminatory Practice*, 3rd edn. Basingstoke: Palgrave Macmillan.

Tompsett, H., Henderson, K., Mathew Byrne, J., Gaskell Mew, E. and Tompsett, C. (2017) On the learning journey: what helps and hinders the development of social work students' core pre-placement skills?, *Social Work Education*, 36(1): 6–25. DOI: 10.1080/02615479.2016.1249836.

Trotter, C. (2015) *Working with Involuntary Clients: A Guide to Practice*, 3rd edn. Sydney: Allen & Unwin.

TUC (Trades Union Congress) (2019a) *Tackling Third-Party Abuse and Harassment: A Guide for Trade Union Reps*. London: TUC. Available at: https://www.tuc.org.uk/resource/tackling-third-party-abuse-and-harassment (accessed 5.03.20).

TUC (Trades Union Congress) (2019b) *Still Just a Bit of Banter? Sexual Harassment in the Workplace in 2016*. London: TUC. Available at: https://www.tuc.org.uk/sites/default/files/SexualHarassmentreport2016.pdf (accessed 5.03.20).

TUC (Trades Union Congress) (2019c) *Sexual harassment of LGBT people in the workplace*. Available at: https://www.tuc.org.uk/research-analysis/reports/sexual-harassment-lgbt-people-workplace (accessed 24.04.20).

Tuck, V. (2013) Resistant parents in child protection: knowledge base, pointers for practice, and implications for policy, *Child Abuse Review*, 22(1): 5–20.

Vuckovic, M., Floyd, B. and Riley, J. (2019) The first year colloquium: creating a safe space for students to flourish, *Journal of the Scholarship of Teaching and Learning*, 19(2): 172–86.

Vygotsky, L.S. (1964) Thought and language, *Annals of Dyslexia*, 14(1): 97–8.

Watts, L. (2019) Reflective practice, reflexivity, and critical reflection in social work education in Australia, *Australian Social Work*, 72(1): 8–20.

Wilson, K., Ruch, G., Lymbery, M. and Cooper, A. (eds) (2011) *Social Work: An Introduction to Contemporary Practice*, 2nd edn. Harlow: Pearson Education.

Winnicott, D.W. (1965) *The Maturational Process and the Facilitating Environment*. New York: International Universities Press.

World Health Organization (2018) *Elder abuse*. Available at: https://www.who.int/news-room/fact-sheets/detail/elder-abuse (accessed 24.04.20).

Index

Page numbers in *italics* refer to tables.